Patrick O'Kane is a in-house barrister with a large multinational organisation. Patrick is also the author of the books 'GDPR: Fix it Fast – How to Apply GDPR to your company in ten steps' and 'A Practical Guide to GDPR in Financial Services'. He has written on Privacy for numerous journals and magazines.

A Practical Guide to Managing GDPR Data Subject Access Requests

Second Edition

A Practical Guide to Managing GDPR Data Subject Access Requests
Second Edition

Patrick O'Kane

Law Brief Publishing

Published 2022 by Law Brief Publishing, an imprint of Law Brief Publishing Ltd
30 The Parks
Minehead
Somerset
TA24 8BT

www.lawbriefpublishing.com

Paperback: 978-1-914608-54-4

For Katherine

PREFACE

We live in the Information Age. A world where over 5 billion people use the internet. An inter-connected world where billions of emails, WhatsApp messages and texts bounce around the globe daily. A recent newspaper article estimated that more than 2.5 quintillion bytes of data are generated on earth every day; more data than all the words spoken by all the human beings who ever existed.

Personal data are all around us. Fortunately, we have rights over this data.

The right to access your personal data is a powerful right. Under the EU General Data Protection Regulation ('GDPR'), individuals can request access to, and a copy of, their personal data. This is known as a 'Data Subject Access Request', an 'Access Request' or a 'DSAR'. As this Guide will explain the rules on Access Requests continue to apply in the UK after Brexit. Dealing with Access Rights can be costly. A recent study showed that UK businesses can pay up to £336,000 per month dealing with customer Access Requests.

An individual can assert this right against any organisation that holds their personal data, from Facebook to their local doctor. The individual can also demand that the organisation answer some tough questions about the personal data such as where they obtained it and who they shared it with. Companies that breach the rules on Access Requests can be subject to fines, litigation and reputational damage.

Access Requests can often put companies on the back foot. Indeed, the Right of Access has become increasingly 'weaponised' by customers involved in disputes with companies. Individuals often assert the Right of Access to put pressure on companies with whom they are having a dispute.

This is a practical guide. It sets out the steps you can take to put your organisation on the right side of GDPR Access Requests.

I do refer to the UK Data Protection Regulator, the Information Commissioner's Office (ICO), throughout the text.

The legal references within this book are accurate as of 17 August 2022.

Patrick O'Kane
August 2022

CONTENTS

CHAPTER ONE
WHAT IS AN ACCESS
REQUEST?

Introduction

In this chapter, we look at some of the basic concepts and definitions as they relate to Access Requests.

A Data Subject Access Request (which I will refer to as an 'Access Request' throughout the book for ease of reference) is a right to access personal data under Article 15 of the EU General Data Protection Regulation (GDPR).[1]

Individuals have a right to obtain a copy of their personal data as well as other supplementary information. It helps people understand how your company is using their data and whether you are doing so lawfully.

For example, Clare has an argument with her solicitor about the fees she was charged for her conveyance. She believes her solicitor has overcharged her for the work performed. She sends her solicitor an email asking to see copies of all the personal information the solicitor holds about her. Clare has made an Access Request.

We discuss these concepts in more detail within the book.

Access Requests only entitle individuals to see their personal data. Individuals do not have a right to see non-personal data under the Right of Access.

---

[1] GDPR – Article 15(1)–(4)

What is GDPR?

The General Data Protection Regulation (GDPR) is an EU Regulation which regulates the processing of personal data. The GDPR applies to companies processing personal data if those companies are either:

1. In the EU or

2. Outside the EU but:

    a. offering goods or services to individuals in the EU or

    b. monitoring the behaviour of those individuals in the EU (for example, by tracking their online behaviour).[2]

Both Processors and Controllers (see below) are caught by GDPR if they fall into 1. or 2. Above.

GDPR grants individuals in the EU a number of Rights including the Right to Access, Erase and even Rectify their personal data.

Does GDPR still apply in the UK?

Yes. GDPR is still part of UK law as 'UK GDPR'. In practice, UK GDPR is virtually identical to the original EU GDPR save for some minor amendments. After Brexit, the UK can set some of its own rules relating to Data Protection law. However, most of the legal principles, including those relating to Access Requests, remain the same. The UK GDPR operates together with the UK Data Protection Act 2018 ('DPA 2018'). The DPA 2018 and UK GDPR are the framework for data protection law in the UK

The UK Data Protection and Digital Information Bill (published in July 2022) which has not yet passed into law, may make some

---

[2] GDPR – Article 3

amendments to the rules on Access Requests. Under this bill, companies may have more power to refuse vexatious requests.

Who does UK GDPR apply to?

1. UK GDPR applies to organisations in the UK that process the personal data of individuals.

2. UK GDPR also applies to organisations based outside the UK if their processing activities relate to:

   - offering goods or services to individuals in the UK; or

   - monitoring the behaviour of individuals in the UK.

As the ICO has said '*There are also implications for UK controllers who have an establishment in the EEA, have customers in the EEA, or monitor individuals in the EEA. The EU GDPR still applies to this processing*'.

What is the Data Protection Act 2018?

The Data Protection Act 2018 (DPA 2018) is a UK Law which supplements and amplifies GDPR in the UK in a number of areas including in the area of Access Requests. GDPR allows national laws to include some exemptions or exceptions to GDPR. The DPA 2018 implements some of those exemptions including in the area of Access Requests. These exemptions are discussed in more detail in Chapter 9.

What is the ICO?

The Information Commissioner's Officer (ICO) regulates data protection in the UK. The ICO deals with complaints from the public about their data are processed. The ICO have the power to conduct audits of companies, and can take enforcement action against companies for breach of law and regulation including GDPR. The largest fine the ICO has imposed to date is £20 million imposed against an airline for a data breach incident.

What is personal data?

The right of access relates to "personal data".

Article 4(1) of GDPR states that 'personal data' means:

- any information

- relating to an identified or identifiable natural person ('data subject').

For ease of reference I sometimes use the word 'data' in this book when I am referring to personal data.

What is an identifiable person?

Personal data is information that relates to an identified or identifiable natural person.[3]

Sometimes, we can identify someone directly from the personal data, for example, from their full name.

On other occasions, we may not be able to identify the person directly from the data on its own. However, we may be able to identify the person from the data by linking it to other data or through making further enquiries.

For example, we might have an email in which an employee ID number is mentioned. On its own, the ID number does not reveal anything. However, when enquiries are made it transpires that the

---

[3]   GDPR – Article 4(1)

4

employee number belongs to Sharon, a Doctor with London Medical. The ID number is therefore Sharon's personal data. We could not identify Sharon directly from the ID number on its own, but we could identify her indirectly (i.e. after making further enquiries). Therefore, the ID number is personal data.

What kinds of information can be personal data?

Personal data can come in a variety of forms. Remember, personal data is:

- any information

- relating to an identified or identifiable natural person ('data subject').

For example, David works as a manager at Silver Bank. He has been there for 15 years. Silver holds a lot of David's personal data including:

a) His name and address

b) Location data relating to David

c) Information about his performance at work

d) Opinions about David expressed by his colleagues in emails

e) David's sickness record

f) CCTV footage of David entering and leaving the building

g) Call records of conversations David had with Human Resources

h) Details of David's browsing history at work

All of these things at A. – H. are David's personal data because they:

1. Are data or information and

2. They relate to David.

Wide interpretation of personal data

The GDPR definition of personal data is very wide. Virtually any data that relates to an individual is likely to be their personal data.

What is a data subject?

The human being to whom the personal data relates. The data subject has the right to make a Data Subject Access Request.

What is a Controller?

A Controller the entity in control of the personal data. Specifically, he Controller is the organisation that 'determines the purposes and means of the processing of personal data'.[4] In other words, they decide how and why the person's personal data is processed.[5] If your company is a Controller, then they must comply with the Access Requests they receive from their employees, customers and anyone on whom they hold personal data.

What are Joint Controllers?

Joint Controllers are 'two or more controllers jointly determining the purposes and means of the processing'.[6] For example, two law firms working together on behalf of the same client on the same case could be joint controllers.

---

[4]   GDPR – Article 4(7)

[5]   GDPR – Article 4(7)

[6]   GDPR – Article 26(1)

What is a Processor?

'Processor' means a natural or legal person, public authority, agency or other body which processes personal data on behalf of the controller.[7] Processors must do what they are told with the personal data.

Many companies use third parties to help them carry out their business operations, for example, IT support businesses, couriers, payroll services, waste disposal etc.

If Company A is hired by Company B to help it with its operations, then that company **may** be a Processor depending on the nature of the agreement between them. If Company B is given no autonomy over the personal data they are processing as part of the agreement, then Company B is a Processor. Processors must do what they are told with the personal data they receive from the Controller.

Processors must be careful not to step outside their instructions from the Controller. If they do, they may become a Controller.[8]

For example, Bling Car Sales use E-Z Payroll to process their employee payroll data. Bling is a Controller for Bling's 's employee personal data and E-Z is a Processor in respect of Bling's employee personal data.

Do all companies caught by GDPR need to comply with Access Requests?

No. Controllers must comply with Access Requests. Controllers are the companies that bear the ultimate legal responsibility for the data processing under GDPR.

---

[7] GDPR – Article 4(8)

[8] GDPR – Article 4(8)

Can Processors ignore DSAR requests?

No. Processors may have responsibilities under their contract with the Controller to assist the Controller with Access Requests they receive. For example, the Processor might be storing or holding the individual's data on the Controller's behalf. The Controller may need assistance from the Processor in locating that data so the Controller can send it to the individual.[9]

For example, as we said above, Bling Car Sales use E-Z Payroll to process their employee payroll data. Bling is a Controller for the firm's employee data and E-Z is a Processor. Bling receive an Access Request from Jim, a trainee Sales Manager at Bling. Jim wants access to all of his personal data. Some of Jim's data is held by E-Z. Bling reach out to E-Z to ask them for a copy of the payroll data. They add that to the other data they hold on Jim and they send it on to Jim.

What does 'processing' personal data mean?

Processing means "any operation or set of operations which is performed on personal data".[10] Doing anything with personal data including deleting it or storing it falls under the definition of processing.

What are the special categories of personal data?

There are certain categories of personal data that require extra protection under GDPR. These categories of personal data are known as the special categories of personal data. They are sometimes referred to as 'sensitive personal data'.

The special categories are personal data 'relating to revealing racial or

---

[9]   GDPR – Article 28(3)(e)

[10]   GDPR – Article 4(2)

ethnic origin, political opinions, religious or philosophical beliefs, or trade union membership, and the processing of genetic data, biometric data for the purpose of uniquely identifying a natural person, data concerning health or data concerning a natural person's sex life or sexual orientation'.[11]

The more sensitive the data, the more it is incumbent on the Controller to put appropriate security in place around the personal data.[12]

The potential consequences of failing to comply with GDPR Access Request obligations

There are three potential consequences:

i) **A Regulatory Sanction** – Breach of the rules on Access Requests can lead to a fine. The maximum fine under UK GDPR is up to £17.5 million or 4% of total worldwide annual turnover, whichever is higher, although fines levied by Regulators must be 'proportionate'.[13] Failing to comply with Access Requests may not mean that your company is fined but it may encourage a Regulator to investigate your company or even issue another regulatory sanction such as an Enforcement Notice.[14] In 2021/2022, 37% of the complaints received by the Information Commissioner's Office related to Access Requests.[15]

ii) **Legal action** – Any person who suffers damage as a result of a breach of any of their GDPR rights can sue the Controller or

---

[11] GDPR – Article 9(1)

[12] GDPR – Article 32

[13] GDPR – Article 83(5)

[14] Data Protection Act 2018 – s149-153

[15] ICO Annual Report 2020–2021

Processor for compensation.[16] In other words, they can sue if their Data Subject Access Request is ignored or not fully complied with.

If a person's Access Rights are not upheld, then the person can:

7. Apply to court for an order forcing the Controller to comply with the Access Request and/or

8. Sue for compensation for breach of the person's subject access rights.

iii) **Criminal Offence** – In some cases, failing to comply with the law on Access Requests can be a criminal offence. It is a criminal offence to alter, deface, block, erase, destroy or conceal information with the intention of preventing disclosure of all or part of the information that the person making the Access Request would have been entitled to receive.[17]

---

[16] GDPR Article 82(1)

[17] Data Protection Act 2018 – s173.

CHAPTER TWO
WHICH CATEGORIES
OF DATA CAN A
PERSON ACCESS?

Introduction

In this chapter, we look at Access Requests in more detail including whether a person's motive in making the request is relevant. We also discuss the types of data that can be accessed.

Under an Access Request, an individual can ask any organisation whether they hold personal data about them. They can also request a copy of that personal data.

In some cases, they may ask for a specific type of personal data. For example, they may say something like "Please send me my emails from November 2019".

There are ways of potentially narrowing an Access Request that we will discuss further in Chapter 3.

In Part 1 of this Chapter, we discuss whether you should provide a copy of the documents on which the personal data is held or whether it is more appropriate to provide a transcript of that personal data.

In Part 2 of this Chapter, we discuss what to do when someone makes a request for Supplementary Information.

What is the Supplementary Information?

Under the Access Request Rules, an individual can ask for further details about their personal data processing. This further information is known as the Supplementary Information. Under the

Supplementary Information rules, the requestor can ask a number of questions including who you share their data with and how long you keep their data. They may also ask for details about the source of their personal data. The company dealing with the request must answer those questions as well as sending out a copy of the personal data. In practice, this does not happen very often. Usually, a person will be satisfied by receiving a copy of their personal data.

Being careful about what you put in writing

We should be aware that any personal data contained in emails could potentially be disclosable under a Subject Access Request including opinions expressed by the requestor. If you do wish to communicate something very sensitive about an individual but are concerned about committing it to writing, then it is advisable to use the phone rather than putting it in an email.

If you were to remember one thing from this book, then perhaps it should be this: Be very careful about what you put in emails. Emails can exist in perpetuity and any comments you do make could be subject to a future Access Request.

Access to, and a copy of, the personal data

Under GDPR, individuals are entitled to obtain 'access to' [18] and 'a copy of the personal data'[19]. A Controller cannot refuse to provide personal data to a person because they believe the person already has the data.

---

[18] GDPR – Article 15(1)

[19] GDPR – Article 15(3)

Paper records

GDPR does not apply to unstructured paper records so if your firm holds unstructured paper records (for example, loose leaf handwritten notes at the bottom of your desk drawer), then strictly speaking, they are not subject to the rules on Access Requests.[20] If the paper records are part of a filing system such as paper files stored in a filing cabinet in alphabetical order, then they are subject to the rules on Access Requests.

Motive is irrelevant

The motive of the person making the Access Request is irrelevant[21]. For example, a former client may be ill-motivated towards a Law Firm and decide to make an Access Request. They may also be making the request because they are contemplating litigation against the firm. Their motivation in making the request is basically irrelevant and does not impede their right to access their personal data.

Should you supply the requestor with an explanation of the personal data?

Personal data provided to a requestor should be provided in a concise, transparent, intelligible, and easily accessible form, using clear and plain language.[22]

Often, it may suffice to provide the individual with a copy of the documents. On some occasions, it may be necessary to explain aspects of the personal data to the requestor. For example, codes or acronyms or poor handwriting within the personal data should be explained to the individual.

---

[20] GDPR – Article 2(1), 4(6)

[21] Dawson-Damer & Ors v Taylor Wessing LLP [2017] EWCA Civ 4

[22] GDPR – Article 12(1)

Part 1

Sending copies of the documents usually works

In most cases, when you receive an Access Request, sending a copy of the documents to the requestor will work best.

However, sometimes personal data in documents is mixed up with other data. The other data might be company non-personal data such as sales figures or share prices etc. If this data is not personal data, then it does not have to be released as part of an Access Request. The other data might be personal data belonging to a different person (we discuss this in more detail in Chapter 5). Remember that we only have to provide the requestor's personal data when we receive an Access Request from them. We are not obliged to release non-personal data. For example, if Person A writes to Company B and says 'I want to make an Access Request under GDPR for all my personal data including details of Company B's 2022 annual report' then Company B are obliged to release Person A's data to him but they do not have to disclose the annual report to him.

One UK Access Request legal case (Guriev v Community Safety Development (UK)Ltd [2016] EWHC 47) states *"the requirement to provide a copy of the data.... can be satisfied by the provision of redacted copy documents, but that is not the only way. Another is a transcript of the data."*

As an alternative to providing a copy of the documents, then you may:

- Provide a transcript of the data, or

- Take the personal data relating to the requestor and put it into a different document or file rather than providing a copy of the documents.

For example:

- Margaret is a client of Red Marketing.

- She makes an Access Request for all of her personal data.

- When preparing her request, Red find a document with Margaret's name along with the fact she paid the firm £1,000 in fees in 2019.

- The document contains similar details of 50 other clients.

- Instead of providing Margaret with a copy of the original document and redacting the other 50 names, Red are allowed to take the data from the document relating to Margaret and place it into a new document.

- In the new shorter document, Red say *"we found a further document containing your name and the fact that you paid £1,000 in fees to us in 2019"*.

Part 2 – Supplementary Information

Supplementary Information – Are people entitled to other information when they make an Access Request?

Yes. Requestors can ask for Supplementary Information when they make an Access Request under Article 15 (1) and (2) of GDPR[23].

In the author's experience, people do not often ask for the Supplementary Information when they make an Access Request.

However, if they do ask for all or any of the supplementary details set out at a) – i) below, then you must provide them with the answers to

---

[23] GDPR – Article 15(1),(2)

those questions along with the rest of the data or documents that you are providing in response to the Access Request.

For example, Alison makes an Access Request to her dentist. She asks for a copy of all her personal data. She also asks for some supplementary information. In particular, Alison asks for details relating to the retention period (see #4. Below) i.e. how long the dentist will be retaining Alison's personal data. Alison's dentist must provide her with a copy of her personal data and also details relating to how long the data are retained.

Which supplementary information are people allowed to see?

In addition to a copy of their personal data, people are also allowed to receive details on:

1. the purposes of your processing i.e. why you are doing the processing

2. the categories of personal data concerned i.e. what kinds of personal data elements you are processing

3. the recipients or categories of recipient to whom the personal data have been or will be disclosed i.e. information about who you are sharing the personal data with

4. your retention period for storing the personal data or, where this is not possible, your criteria for determining how long you will store it i.e. how long you are keeping the personal data before deleting it

5. the existence of their right to request rectification, erasure or restriction or to object to such processing i.e. the other rights they are entitled to assert under GDPR (See Chapter 8)

6. the right to lodge a complaint with the ICO or another supervisory authority

7. information about the source of the data, where it was not obtained directly from the individual i.e. where or from who, you obtained the data

8. the existence of automated decision-making (including profiling) i.e. whether any computer is making a decision about the data subject

9. the safeguards you provide if you transfer personal data to a third country or international organisation i.e. whether you are sending the personal data outside the EU or UK and what you are doing to ensure this data transfer is within the GDPR rules

You may be providing much of this information already in your internet privacy notice and your internet privacy notice may be a good place to start in answering some of the questions above.

Automated decision making

There are obligations within GDPR to disclose information about the existence of automated decision-making (including profiling) where that decision making has a significant effect on the requestor, including the logic behind the automated decision making and the consequences for the requestor.

For example, Asha applies for a job with New Books. Her application is unsuccessful. She learns that her job application was reviewed and rejected by a New Books computer program. She makes an Access Request and specifically requests that New Books explain:

- The logic behind the program i.e. why the program that rejected Asha's application works and

- The consequences for Asha. For example, in future, if Asha applies for such jobs with New Books, will she be prejudged based on her initial result?

If your firm does rely on a computer program to make decisions like this, then you may wish to draft a statement that explains this fact to individuals.

Do I have to provide the Supplementary Information above in categories a) – i) every time I receive an Access Request?

Often a person will request 'all' of their personal data without specifically requesting the supplementary information set out at categories a) – i) above.

Some consider it best practice to always include the Supplementary Information when a person requests 'all' of their personal data. However, it is reasonable to provide the supplementary information only if this is specifically asked for by the requestor.

Example of providing the Supplementary Information at a) – i) above.

David is a client at a firm called Cookstown Lawyers. He heard from his friend that Cookstown's computer systems were hacked. David is curious about the personal data that Cookstown have on him, and he decides to make an Access Request. He emails Cookstown Lawyers and says that he wants to see all of his personal data. Also, he has asked for the supplementary information at a) – i) above.

Criminal send David a copy of all the personal data they hold on him. It is contained in a secure file.

They also send him a table containing the Supplementary information that David has asked for:

Further Supplementary Information Requested by David in his Access Request to Criminal Lawyers	Details of Cookstown Lawyers' response to David on the points he has raised
1. The purposes of their processing	• To perform our contract with you • To administer payments • To allow you to use our website • To send you marketing • To defend legal claims you take against us Please see our Internet Privacy Policy for more details.
2. The categories of personal data concerned	• Name • Address • Email address • Browsing information from our website • Payment information • Details relating to your case Please see our Internet Privacy Policy for more details.

3. The recipients or categories of recipient you disclose the personal data to e.g. employee, agent, processor	We share personal data with: • IT support providers • Payment processing and debt collection services • Marketing companies Please see our Internet Privacy Policy for more details.
4. Your retention period for storing the personal data	We store your personal data for a further five years after the conclusion of your case. After that, we delete the personal data. Please see our Internet Privacy Policy for more details.
5. The existence of the right to request rectification, erasure or restriction or to object to such processing	You do have a right to correct, erase or stop the processing of your personal data in certain circumstances. Please see our Internet Privacy Policy for more details on how to make these requests.
6. The right to lodge a complaint with the ICO or another supervisory authority.	You do have a right to lodge a complaint about the way in which we process your personal data with a supervisory authority. Please see our Internet Privacy Policy for more details on how to make such a complaint.

7. The information about the source of the data, where it was not obtained directly from the individual. N.B. basic information on the source will usually suffice. You do not need to include "every hand through which the data has passed."[24]	We received your personal data from: • When you contact us • When you attended our office and gave us instructions about your case • When you browse our site, cookies collect data about you • Third parties including debt recovery and fraud protection when setting up your account or seeking payment of our fees Please see our Internet Privacy Policy for more details.
8. The existence of automated decision-making (including profiling).	We do not carry out any automated decision- making when processing your personal data.
9. The safeguards you provide if you transfer personal data to a third country or international organisation.	When we send your personal data outside the UK or EU, we make sure that the receiving party has agreed to our standard contract clauses to ensure they handle your data in a safe and secure manner. Please see our Internet Privacy Policy for more details.

---

[24] Johnson v Medical Defence Union [2007] EWCA Civ 262

The answers above are only examples. If you are asked for the Supplementary Information at a) – i), then you must check the answers to each of these questions in relation to your own company. Much of this information may appear in your Internet Privacy Policy which should set out how and why you use the requestor's personal data. Looking at your Company's Internet Privacy Policy is a good place to start in dealing with these questions.

Recap

- Be careful what you write in emails. It may be subject to a future Access Request.

- Individuals are entitled to access to and a copy of their personal data.

- A person's motive in making an Access Request is irrelevant.

- Sending copies of original documents containing the personal data usually works but you can potentially place the data into a new document to send to the individual.

- People can ask for supplementary information as well as the data such as details about where your company obtained their personal data.

CHAPTER THREE
ACCESS REQUESTS:
THE FORMALITIES

Introduction

In this chapter we set out some of the basic rules on Access Requests including:

- Time limits

- A useful rule in narrowing the request

- ID checks

- Refusing to answer certain requests

Does an Access Request have to be made in a particular format?

No. Access Requests can be made orally or in writing. Most are made by email.

If it is clear that the requestor is asking for a copy of their own personal information, the requestor does **not** have to

- Send the request to a particular person within your organisation such as the Data Protection Officer

- Use the term Data Subject Access Request or DSAR

- Mention GDPR

- Use your form or webform to submit their request (they can make the request in the way they want to make it i.e. by sending an email to your company and they do not have to use your process)

A person can make an Access Request to your company by requesting their information:

1. On a telephone call with you

2. Via email

3. In a social media message such as a Tweet or a Direct Message on Twitter

4. In a letter

5. In a voicemail message

6. Through a third party who makes Access Requests on behalf of individuals (See at 'Agents' below)

Websites that offer to make Access Requests on behalf of individuals are becoming increasingly popular.

Recognising an Access Request

There is a legal obligation on all companies to recognise Access Requests when they are made. Organisations must train staff to recognise and act upon access requests when they are made by customers, staff and employees.

There is no form of words required to make an Access Request. Sometimes, individuals mistakenly refer to an Access Request as a 'Freedom of Information Request'.

If you run a company and a client asks on the phone for "a copy of all my data" then staff should be adequately trained to recognise this as an Access Request and to escalate it to the correct person within your organisation.

The key is that all of your employees who interact with individuals, such as clients, have some form of specific training on how to recognise Access Requests.

If you don't recognise a request and this leads to you failing to deal with an Access Request adequately or in time, then you are in breach of GDPR and may be fined by a Regulator or even sued for damages as a result of the delay.[25]

Can we demand that the requestor completes an Access Request form or uses our process?

No. There is no requirement on the requestor to complete a form before something is recognised as an Access Request. You can request that the requestor completes your form. But you cannot force them to do so.

Must we always treat a request for data or a document as an Access Request?

Not necessarily. Sometimes, it is not necessary to kick off the formal Access Request process. Companies are often asked by customers to provide documents in the normal course of business.

For example, if a customer says "Please send me the three emails I received from you last March 25" or "Please re-send me the letter you sent to me from 15 April", then you may be able to do this simply and instantly. You can send the emails or resend the letter without kicking off the Access Request process.

If they do ask for "all my data" or for a substantial amount of data,

---

[25] AB v Ministry of Justice [2014] EWHC 1847 (QB)

such as "all of my email correspondence with you since 2017", then it will be more appropriate to deal with the matter as an Access Request.

IMPORTANT: **Encouraging individuals to narrow their access request**

There is a way in which you can ask a requestor to narrow their Access Request. Sometimes, it is not clear what a requestor is asking for, or indeed what they want. In this case, you can ask the requestor for more details.

For example:

- John has worked as a lawyer for Big Law for 25 years.

- Big Law hold 100,000 emails containing John's personal data.

- John makes an Access Request for copies his personal data after he was made redundant.

- Big Law email John and ask him to clarify his request and to specify which documents he wants.

- Luckily for Big Law, John confirms that he is only seeking copies of his emails from March 2021, the month before he was made redundant.

- Big Law are relieved and they provide John with a copy of these emails from March 2021.

- They do not need to search through the remaining 25 years of emails.

- Clarifying the request has saved Big Law time and money.

GDPR says *"Where the controller processes a large quantity of information concerning the data subject, the controller should be able to request that, before the information is delivered, the data subject specify the information or processing activities to which the request relates.*"[26]

You can ask the requestor to give you more specifics about the personal data they are seeking including:

- **The types of documents they want** e.g. my emails with your company.

- **The types of processing** e.g. any information relating to my billing records.

- **The time period relating to the data sought** e.g. from March 2016 until March 2017.

If the requestor refuses to play ball on this issue, then you must proceed on and deal with the Access Request as best you can. You can ask them to narrow the request and ask for specifics in terms of a) – c) above but they will not always co-operate with you.

Is the time limit for dealing with the request affected by the request for clarification?

The ICO has said:

> *"If you process a large amount of information about an individual, you may ask them to specify the information or processing activities their request relates to before responding to the request. The time limit for responding to the request is paused until you receive clarification. This is referred to as 'stopping the clock'."*

---

[26] GDPR – Recital 63

Identity Checks

When you receive an Access Request, you must be careful to verify that the person you are dealing with is who they claim to be. Put simply, if you receive an Access Request from one of your company clients called David A. Williams, then you must verify that the person contacting you is David A. Williams and not someone who is merely pretending to be David A. Williams.

The BBC News site reported a case where a University of Oxford researcher decided to conduct an experiment on Access Requests.[27] He contacted 83 companies pretending to be his fiancée. His fiancée had agreed to participate in the experiment and allowed him to see if he could obtain her data from various companies. Of the 83 companies he contacted:

1. 24% supplied personal information without verifying the requestor's identity.

It is crucial that you properly check the identity of the requestor. Otherwise, you could find yourself in a position where you have sent out personal data to a fraudster, which would mean that you have breached GDPR Data Security rules.[28]

What is the test for checking someone's identity?

Under Article 12(6) of GDPR, where the controller has reasonable doubts concerning the identity of the requestor, they may request the provision of additional information necessary to confirm the identity of the data subject.

The identity checks also ensure that you can locate the data relating to that person. For example, you may have more than two customers

---

[27] https://www.bbc.co.uk/news/technology-49252501

[28] GDPR – Article 5 and 32

called Kate Lowe. The Kate Lowe making the request has a DOB of 1.1.1985. The identity checks will help you find the data relating to this Kate Lowe and not the other Kate Lowe.

What kind of proof of identity should I ask for?

You should ask for any "additional information necessary" if you have "reasonable doubts" about the person's identity.[29]

If you have had a previous relationship with the person, then an email or even a signed letter will usually be enough.

For example, Roger T. Moore has worked for London Tours for 20 years. His HR Department receive an Access Request from his email address Roger.Moore@LondonTours.com. Depending on the circumstances, further proof of identity may not be needed. In this case, London Tours are confident that the request is genuine and that it comes from Roger T Moore. Roger has been an employee with London Tours for 20 years and his email address is well known to the company.

However, where you need further proof of someone's identity, you should ask for more formal evidence of identity. For example, you might ask for one or more of the following:

- A copy of the person's driving licence or passport

- A copy of a utility bill with the person's name and address, such as a gas or an electricity bill

- Information that only the requestor would know such as an account number or something that the person recently bought from your company

---

[29] GDPR – Article 12(6)

If you have any doubts about the person's identity, then you should make sure you have received adequate evidence of identity before sending any personal data out to the requestor.

Remember that reasonable adjustments must be made for people with disabilities. Companies must ask for "reasonable" verification and not make this too difficult for requestors.

Consistency

It is helpful to have an internal staff policy for your company to enable you to deal with Access Requests. This policy sets out the rules of the game for staff dealing with Access Requests. This policy might set out the manner in which you set out the ID required.

Please see these examples below (NB they are only examples and you may require more stringent means of verification for individuals making Access Requests to your company)

Type of requestor	Means of Verification
☐ Client	• Customer ID; or • Account number; and • Utility Bill
☐ Individual with whom we have no direct relationship e.g. a marketing prospect or a third-party individual on whom we hold personal data	• Copy of driving licence or passport; and • Utility Bill with individual's name and address

☐ Former Employee	• Employee ID; and • Former employee email address; and • Employment dates (start and end)
☐ Current Employee	• Email Access Request; and • Follow up phone call to check

These are only suggestions. Remember that the key role in identity checks is that they are reasonable. Never send personal data out to anyone if you have doubts about their identity.

Within one month – Time Limits for dealing with Access Requests

Under GDPR, we must provide the individual with their data "without undue delay" and at the very least "within one month" of receiving the Access Request. Remember, it is "within one month", not "one month". Try to deal with Access Requests on the day before the "one month" period expires. For example, if an Access Request is made on 14th February, then ensure the individual receives their data by 13th March.

The "within one month" period is a backstop; if you can provide the personal data more quickly than this, then you should do so as GDPR says that Access Requests should be granted "without undue delay".[30]

---

[30] GDPR – Article 12(3)

What happens to the time limit when I have asked for proof of identity?

The ICO has said "The timescale for responding to an Access Request does not begin until you have received the requested information."[31]

For example:

- Gita makes an Access Request on 1 March of her former school, Old School.

- Old School reply on 2nd March seeking verification of Gita's identity.

- They ask Gita to send them a copy of her driving licence and also a copy of a recent electricity bill showing her home address.

- Gita does not provide the ID until 20 March.

- Old School must comply with the request within one month of 20 March at the very latest.

Can the "within one month" Time Limit be extended?

The "within one month" time limit "may be extended by two further months where necessary, taking into account the complexity and number of requests".[32]

It can be extended "where necessary". This means that your company will need a very good reason for seeking to rely on the extension of the time limit i.e. only where it is necessary to do so. A company cannot extend the time limit because it is convenient. It must be a necessity

---

[31] ICO – Right of Access Guidance, October 2020, Page 25

[32] GDPR – Article 12(3)

to extend the time limit.

To extend the time limit, the company must consider the "complexity and number of requests". Examples of potential extensions might be Access Requests that:

- Involve large amounts of data. For example, an employee Access Request with many thousands of emails that are intertwined with the personal data of many other employees and require complex redaction or editing.

- Involve difficult legal issues such as issues relating to a child's Access Request or data that falls within the exceptions to Access Requests (see Chapter 9).

- Involve data that is hard to find. For example, the data may have been archived or it may sit on many separate systems and platforms all over the world.

- Includes multiple requests. For example, an individual might come back several times, changing or updating or adding to the request.

The company shall inform the requestor of "any such extension within one month of receipt of the request, together with reasons for the delay".

A template letter advising the individual that the Access Request will be delayed, which you may find helpful, appears in Appendix 1 at the end of the book.

Can we charge a fee for Access Requests?

Not usually.

Where an Access Request if manifestly unfounded or excessive then your organisation may charge a fee for the administrative costs of

Access Requests under Article 12(5) of GDPR. 4

You may find that charging fees for Access Requests are more trouble than they are worth.

How often can a person make an Access Request?

A person is entitled to exercise their right of access 'at reasonable intervals'.[33]

Can lawyers or other agents make Data Subject Access Requests on behalf of individuals?

Yes. There is no rule against an agent making a request on behalf of the requestor. For example, a lawyer may send a letter from their firm advising that they wish to make an Access Request on their requestor client's behalf. If you do receive such a letter, then you do not need to carry out any identity checks and can assume the lawyer has the authority to make the Access Request. [34]

If you receive an Access Request from any other non-lawyer agent such as a website specialising in making such requests for clients, then you should proceed to ask the agent for evidence that they have the authority to act on behalf of the requestor. You might ask them for a letter of authority from the client or you might ask them to provide identification details for the client, depending on the circumstances.

A third party such as a family member can make an Access Request on behalf of the requestor. The ICO gives the example of a daughter making an Access Request to a bank on behalf of her elderly mother.

---

[33] GDPR – Recital 63

[34] Guriev & Anor v Community Safety Development (UK) Ltd [2016] EWHC 643

In all cases where a third party is making an Access Request on behalf of the requestor, you must be satisfied that the third party has the appropriate authority to make the request on behalf of the requestor. Asking for a signed letter from the requestor along with proof of identity relating to the requestor would be sufficient proof that they have that authority. If you have any doubt regarding the third party's bona fide interest, then you should NOT send the data out.

Can children make Access Requests?

The UK Regulator, the ICO, has said that children can make Access Requests if the controller is confident that they can understand their rights in which case you can respond directly to the child.

A parent can act on behalf of a child to conduct the Access Request if the child does not have sufficient understanding of the Access Request process or if it is in the best interests of the child for the parent to act on their behalf.

Making reasonable adjustments for people with disabilities

In their Subject Access Request Guidance, the ICO says that in line with the Equality Act 2010, you should make reasonable adjustments for people with disabilities to ensure:

- Such persons make Access Requests without difficulty, and

- The data can be delivered in a format which is accessible *"such as large print, audio formats, email or Braille"*.

The ICO goes on to say *"What is a reasonable adjustment will depend on the specific needs of the individual. Before responding to a SAR you should talk to the person to find out how best to meet their needs".* [35]

Can we refuse to answer an Access Request if it is unreasonable?

A company can refuse to act on an Access Request if it is:

    a) manifestly unfounded; or

    b) manifestly excessive.[36]

The Information Commissioner's Office (ICO) in the UK has said that a request may be manifestly unfounded if *"the request is malicious in intent and is being used to harass an organisation with no real purpose other than to cause disruption."*

The ICO have said that to determine whether a request is manifestly excessive, you need to consider whether it is "clearly or obviously unreasonable".[37]

These exceptions are difficult to rely on and they should only be used as a last resort. Your company is best advised to try, in so far as is possible, to proceed and deal with any Access Request they receive. Remember, it is up to you to prove that the request falls into this exception.

In the case of Lees v Lloyds Bank (2020 EWHC 2249), it was found that issuing numerous and repetitive requests can potentially be an abuse of the Access Request process.

If you do decide that you are refusing to act on the request, then you must write to the requestor setting out your reasons for refusing to act.

A template letter advising the individual that the Access Request will

---

[35] ICO – Right of Access Guidance, October 2020, Page 23

[36] GDPR – Article 12(5)

[37] ICO – Right of Access Guidance, October 2020, Page 40

not be acted upon appears in this book at Appendix 1. .

The dangers of amending personal data

An Access Request relates to the data held at the time the request is received. For example, if Davina makes an Access Request to her employer Big Co in March 2022, Davina is entitled to see all of the data that Big Co hold on her at March 2022. However, what happens if Big Co are about to delete much of the company data in March 2022 as part of their ordinary records management and some of this data relates to Davina?

The ICO say:

> *"It is our view that a SAR relates to the data you held at the time you received the request. However, in many cases, routine use of the data may result in it being amended or even deleted while you are dealing with the request. So it is reasonable for you to supply the information you hold when you respond, even if this is different to what you held when you received the request."*

However, it is probably safer to place a hold on the deletion or amendment of the requestor's data as soon as you receive the Access Request as this prevents the requestor from alleging that his data has been purposefully deleted or manipulated in some way. Remember, it is a criminal offence to alter, deface, block, erase, destroy or conceal information with the intention of hiding all or part of the information a person making the Access Request would have been entitled to receive.

How should personal data be sent out?

When you receive the request by email, it is best to reply using secure email. GDPR says "where the data subject makes the request by electronic means, and unless otherwise requested by the data subject, the information shall be provided in a commonly used electronic form."[38]

GDPR suggests that Controllers should, where possible, provide access via a secure portal that gives people direct access to their data.[39]

The key is that the personal data should be sent out securely. Under Article 32 of GDPR, Controllers must take appropriate steps to keep data secure. If a Controller were to send data in an Access Request out improperly or without proper security, then they could be in line for a fine. In 2016, the ICO issued a medical practice with a fine of £40,000 for unlawfully disclosing the personal data of Person A and B in response to an Access Request from Person C.

The ICO has said companies should *"have a system or procedure in place to check email or postal addresses before responding to a request".*[40]

When sending information out via email, then encrypted email and password protected documents should be considered. If the personal data is being sent by post, then recorded delivery should be used.

Somewhat annoyingly, Article 12(1) of GDPR allows individuals to request that their personal data be delivered orally. The author has never seen (or heard!) this done in practice.

Recap:

- The controller can ask the requestor to specify the data they are requesting with respect to specific documents or dates of documents. This is a very useful tool and could save your company time and money if you are able to persuade the requestor to be more specific about the data they are seeking.

---

[38] GDPR – Article 15(3)

[39] GDPR – Recital 63

[40] ICO – Right of Access Guidance, October 2020, Page 36

- In relation to ID, you should ask for any "additional information necessary" if you have "reasonable doubts" about the person's identity.

- The personal data should be provided "within one month" although this may potentially be extended for complex or numerous requests.

- Lawyers can make requests on behalf of clients.

- Children can make Access Requests if their understanding of the situation is sufficient.

- Reasonable adjustments should be made to your Access Requests procedures to take account of people with disabilities.

- Be very careful in amending personal data that is the subject of an Access Request before it goes out.

- Your company can refuse to act on an Access Request if it can show that the Access Request is 'manifestly unfounded' or manifestly excessive'.

CHAPTER FOUR
THE SEARCH

Introduction

In this Chapter we look at how to search for the personal data.

In the digital age, companies hold more data on us now than ever before. In the old days, most or all of the personal data held by a company on a client was often in the client file in a dusty filing cabinet. In the post-GDPR era, companies may hold all sorts of weird and wonderful data relating to their clients, employees and other members of the public. This data might be held by numerous different departments within the company such as the marketing, HR and IT Departments. It may be held by numerous suppliers also such as cloud providers, marketing analytics companies and payroll providers. It could be held across a multiplicity of platforms and systems scattered across the globe. In many cases, companies do not know where their data resides. They may have collected and processed so much that they have lost track of their data. This unknown data is sometimes referred to as 'dark data'.

Who should help you with the search?

When you receive an Access Request, you must assess where the data relating to the requestor resides.

Then, you must approach the appropriate people in your company to help you find that personal data.

In larger firms, it is likely that the IT Department is your first port of call. They can run a search for you to help you find copies of the personal data relating to the requestor. You may decide that HR can help you locate some of the personal data if the requestor is an employee. If a customer has made an Access Request then your marketing department may hold some of the data on the customer.

Some of the data may not be on your own company systems. Your outsourced service Processors may hold personal data on your behalf relating to the requestor. Your Processors may need to help you locate and retrieve this data following receipt of an Access Request. It is important that they provide you with the personal data they hold on you and to give you access to it if you need it. A template letter for reaching out to processors appears at Annex 1.

Preparing now for future requests

When you receive an Access Request, you will have to reach out across your organisation and your suppliers to locate the personal data. It is worth having discussions now about how you would locate personal data relating to one of your employees or your customers. It makes sense to have discussions with your IT Department to see if they have the capacity to locate this data. Also, you may wish to consider purchasing a software tool to help you locate the data you need.

Must I find every scrap of personal data on the requestor if they make an Access Request?

The UK case of Deer v. Oxford University sheds light on this subject[41]. In this case, Lord Justice Lewison said "*the implied obligation to search…is limited to a reasonable and proportionate search….. the result of a search does not necessarily mean that every item of personal data relating to an individual will be retrieved*".

The European Data Protection Board seems to have a somewhat different view. They do see limited constraints on the search that must be conducted and believe that companies must search and find the

---

[41] Deer-v-University of Oxford [2017] EWCA (Civ) 93

data wherever it may reside. The author is surprised at this given the long-standing presence of proportionality in EU law. However, post-Brexit, the ICO is no longer a member of the EDPB.

The ICO has said that you should make reasonable efforts to find and retrieve the requested information. For example, it may be disproportionate to start searching CCTV and call records if there is a minimal chance of finding any personal data relating to the requestor.

This highlights the need for a good Records Management Policy within your firm. If you purge data regularly from your systems, then you will be under less of a burden with Access Requests.

The ICO has said "The burden of proof is on you to be able to justify why a search is unreasonable or disproportionate."[42]

Saving yourself some headaches

As we discussed in the previous chapter it is always useful to try to get the requestor to narrow their search, you can ask the requestor to give you more specifics about the personal data they are seeking including:

- The types of documents they want e.g. my emails with your company.

- The types of processing e.g. any information relating to my billing records.

- The time period relating to the data sought e.g. from March 2016 until March 2017.

Whilst you cannot and should not force the requestor to narrow their search, it is always useful to try to persuade the requestor to narrow their search. Please read the section entitled 'Encouraging individuals

---

[42] ICO Subject Access Request Guidance, page 28

to narrow their access request' in Chapter 3 for more details.

Where should you search?

The search for the requestor's personal data could include a search of all relevant electronic and paper systems:

- Case files

- Marketing data

- Internet logs

- Emails

- Correspondence

- Databases

- Paper files

- Call recordings

- Archived data

- Other documents that mention the Requestor

- Data Analytics data relating to the requestor

It does not matter where in the world the data is stored. The Right of Access applies to personal data stored anywhere in the world.

Paper Records

As we said in Chapter 2, GDPR does not apply to unstructured paper records so if your firm holds unstructured paper records (for example, loose leaf handwritten notes at the bottom of your desk drawer), then strictly speaking, they are not subject to the rules on Access Requests. If the paper records are part of a filing system, then they are subject to the rules on Access Requests.

Handling emails

Emails are particularly difficult because searches can uncover thousands of emails that mention the requestor. In one UK Legal case, an employee made DSARs against their employer. The employer reviewed over 500,000 emails in the course of the search.[43]

Also, it is important to bear in mind that it is not always clear when something amounts to personal data and when it does not in respect of emails.

Dealing with personal data in emails

It is not always clear whether data in an email are personal data. As we have said in Chapter 1, personal data is:

- any information

- relating to an identified or identifiable natural person ('data subject').

It is up to you to judge whether the data in the email is the person's personal data. For example, Dave makes an Access Request to his employer, BigCorp. A large number of emails are found. 30 of these emails are meeting invites to all employees to the Big Corp Monthly Company Drinks receptions from 2017 to 2020. Dave is one of the recipients of the emails. Big Corp decide that meeting invites are not

---

[43] Deer-v-University of Oxford [2017] EWCA (Civ) 121

Dave's personal data.

However, they also uncover 20 emails sent by Dave to the Company Doctor complaining about his anxiety and depression as a result of his job. These emails do contain Dave's personal data.

It is not always clear whether mentioning a person's name in an email constitutes their personal data.

In the Deer case, the judge said (author's underlining):

> "*Accepting as I do that a person's name is his personal data, it does not follow that every piece of information in a document in which his name appears is his personal information.* It would…be enough for the data controller to inform the data subject that, for instance, his name is consistently recorded as Charles Pooter……. in a specified number of documents between particular dates. There would be no obligation to disclose the documents themselves."

Deleted data

Information is deleted when it is permanently discarded and will not be used or accessed again. Data that has been truly deleted is outside the scope of an Access Request. There is a high bar here. If data relating to emails is in a deleted or archived folder, this does not necessarily mean that the personal data is truly "deleted".

Tips when conducting a search for emails

(1) **Software** – Try to ensure software is in place that will allow you to search emails on your central system for the requestor. Use appropriate search terms that are likely to catch as much personal data relating to the requestor as possible such as his name and client number.

(2) **IT** – Ask your IT Department to help you find all of the

references relating to the Requestor.

(3) **Deleted emails** – If any email data is permanently deleted and it could be recovered but there is no intention to try to recover it or use it again, then this does **not** have to be recovered and released under the Access Request rules.

(4) **Archived emails** – Unfortunately, personal data in emails that is archived or that resides in the deletion folder on your live system is still personal data that is subject to the DSAR rules.

What happens after I have located the personal data?

The next part of the process is reviewing the personal data before you send it out. Most companies locate all the emails and documents they have on the requestor. Then they review the documents to see if there are any redactions required before sending the data to the requestor. For example, they may be obliged to remove references to third parties from the data before sending it out (See Chapter 5). Equally, there may be exemptions such as Legal Professional Privilege in play which necessitate further redactions (See Chapter 9). Once the data has been reviewed, it must be sent out securely as discussed in the previous chapter.

Redacting

There are two main ways of redacting information before sending it to a requestor. You can print the documents out and use a black marker to cover the information that must be edited. Alternatively, you can redact the information online by using a software tool that allows you to obscure the relevant information electronically.

Record

It is important to keep a record of the personal data you have sent to the requestor. GDPR requires Controllers to keep appropriate records of their data processing under the Article 5 Accountability Principle. You do not have to retain the records themselves indefinitely but keeping a note of what was sent to the requestor is important in case the requestor ever complains to the ICO about the Access Request. This also helps in case the requestor ever complains.

You may wish to use a table such as this:

Name of Data Subject	Type of Request	Request Ref Number	Requested details	Date Request Received	Date Due	Has ID been verified?	ID documents provided?	Initial response letter?
Bruce Wayne	Access	007	Wants access to emails from March 2019	1.3.20	28.3.20	Yes	Driver's licence	Yes

Recap:

- You must conduct a reasonable search for personal data relating to Access Requests

- This may include paper, electronic records, CCTV footage and other forms of personal data

- Emails are particularly challenging, and you may need help from your IT department and from a software tool to access personal data relating to emails

- You may need assistance from suppliers and other departments within your organisation in order to locate personal data relating to individuals (see Appendix 1 for templates that may assist with these tasks)

CHAPTER FIVE
THIRD PARTY DATA

Introduction

We have now come to perhaps the most challenging part of Access Requests. You have received the request, reached out across your company to find all the data and now you must review it before you send it out.

The problem with personal data is that one person's data is often mixed with another person's personal data. The information sought as part of an Access Request may refer to a third person either directly or indirectly and sometimes you could guess who the third party is in data even if they are not explicitly named.

For example, David is employed at City Lawyers. He sent an email on 1 March to his manager, Paul, complaining about two of his colleagues. He said that Clive, the managing partner, was lazy. He also stated that Angelina, the HR Manager, was incompetent. Paul responded to David's email agreeing with David's comments.

This email chain contains the personal data of four people:

- David – It contains David's name and his opinions about Clive and Angelina.

- Clive – It contains Clive's name and David's opinion about him.

- Angelina – It contains Angelina's name and David's opinion about her.

- Paul – It contains Paul's name and his opinions about Clive and Angelina.

Often emails and other documents contain the personal data of the requestor and other people. I will call the other people 'third parties' for ease of reference.

GDPR (Article 15(4)) says that the right to access your data should not 'adversely affect the rights or freedoms of others'. We must respect the data protection rights of third parties when dealing with Access Requests.[44]

This chapter sets out what we must do when we come across data or documents that contain the personal data of third parties when we are dealing with an Access Request.

Can trade secrets be considered third party information?

Recital 63 of GDPR suggests they can. The Recital says "That right [to access] should not adversely affect the rights or freedoms of others, including trade secrets or intellectual property and in particular the copyright protecting the software."

Can you remove or delete the data relating to the third parties?

When you are dealing with the Access Request, you may find that you can easily remove or delete the data relating to the third parties.

For example, you may be able to do this by:

- **Redacting the third-party data** – Either using a black marker or software to obscure the third party data before sending it to the requestor.

- **Removing the requestor's data and placing it into a new file** – Removing the personal data relating to the requestor and

---

[44] GDPR – Recital 63

placing it into a different document or file.

Redacting or removing personal data is the easiest way of dealing with third party data.

However, in some cases, we may not be able to simply remove the third-party data.

Why can we not just redact or remove the references to third party individuals? Isn't this always the easier option?

Sometimes, it is not possible to delete names or to edit documents and information of third-party individuals.

Example 1: Vanessa is employed at Grim Hotels as the Chief Financial Officer. She was recently turned down for a promotion. Vanessa emails an Access Request to Grim and she specifically asks for a performance review document relating to Vanessa's work performance in 2019. All performance reviews are written up by Louise, the HR Manager at Grim.

The performance review contains Vanessa's data and also the personal data of Louise, the author of the document. It would not make sense to simply redact Louise's name on the document because Vanessa would be able to guess that it refers to Louise. However, the performance review does not reveal a lot about Louise as an individual and it does reveal a substantial amount about Vanessa. It might be better to just send the document to Vanessa, unredacted.

Example 2: Cliff has an argument with his Insurance Company, Gold Cover. He makes an Access Request and, as part of that Access Request, he specifically asks for a call recording relating to a phone call he made on 1 June. On the phone call from 1 June, Cliff had a heated discussion with Terry. Terry is a trainee sales agent at Gold.

The call recording contains Cliff's data and Terry's data but it would be impossible to edit out Terry's voice on the call as it would render the call recording nonsensical.

We have established that it is impossible to remove the third-party data from a particular document. What do we do now?

Once we have decided that we cannot simply delete or edit the third-party data from a specific data set such as a call recording or an email, then you can refuse to release the third-party data unless:

1. The third party has **consented** to the document being released or

2. It is **reasonable** to disclose the third-party data without consent.[45]

Obtaining consent is the best and simplest way to resolve this issue. For example, in Example 2 above, if Gold Cover can get Terry's consent to release the call recording to Cliff, then they can go ahead and release it.

If Terry does not consent to the release of the call recording, then Gold Cover must ask whether it is reasonable to disclose the call recording anyway.

Seeking consent from the third party is not always feasible

Sometimes, it may not be practicable to seek consent. For example, you may not be able to reach the third party or they may be unable to grant legal consent because they are a child or unable to understand the issue sufficiently. Also, it may not be appropriate to seek consent if seeking this consent would reveal too much personal data relating to the requestor.

You must now decide whether it is reasonable to disclose the third-

---

[45] Data Protection Act 2018 – Schedule 2, Part 3 Paragraph 16

party data without consent.

We are unable to obtain consent to release the third-party data. How do we decide if it is reasonable to disclose the third party data?

Let's look at a legal case that looks at this issue.

In the UK case of Dr B v. The General Medical Council,[46] the issue of reasonableness was considered. In this case, a patient complained to the General Medical Council (GMC) about treatment he received from his Doctor. The GMC asked for an independent expert report to be prepared. The GMC sent a summary of the report to the patient. The report contained the Doctor and the patient's personal data. The patient made an Access Request for the full report and the Doctor objected to its disclosure. The Court had to weigh the Privacy rights of the Doctor and the Patient. The Court said it was reasonable for the report to be released to the patient.

The Court said that the Controller must weigh up the rights and interests of the third party when making an assessment on whether to release the third-party personal data. Lord Justice Sales said the controller has a *"wide discretion"* when making such a decision.

As a Controller, you do have a wide discretion in deciding whether it is reasonable to disclose the third-party data.

Other factors to consider in deciding whether it is reasonable to disclose third party data

In deciding whether it is reasonable to release the third-party data, we should consider the following factors in coming to our decision:

---

[46] Dr B v. The General Medical Council 28 June 2018 [2018] EWCA Civ 1497

- **Type of data** – The type of information that you would disclose e.g. the sensitivity of the third party data. Is it something private or something that could cause them embarrassment? The more sensitive the third-party information, the more reasonable it might be to withhold it from the requestor.

- **Confidentiality** – Any duty of confidentiality you owe to the other third party e.g. would the third party expect that the information be kept in confidence, for example, because it is under a Doctor and Patient/Lawyer and Client/Bank and Customer relationship. If the information relating to the third party is under a duty of confidentiality, then you may be able to withhold the information from being disclosed as part of an Access Request. The law on confidentiality is complex so please take legal advice if necessary on this aspect.

- **Consent** – Any steps you have taken to seek consent from the third party i.e. have you asked the third party if they are happy to consent? Also, is this individual capable of giving consent?

- **Refusal of consent** – Any express refusal of consent by the third party i.e. have they refused to give consent? Even if they have refused to give their consent, it still might be appropriate to release the document.[47]

Keeping records

If you do decide not to release personal data relating to third parties, then you should keep a record of your decision so you can explain this at a later stage to a regulator in the event that the requestor makes a complaint about how the Access Request was handled.

---

[47] Data Protection Act 2018 – Schedule 2, Part 3 Paragraph 16

Recap:

Sometimes data relating to an individual making an Access Request is mixed in with data relating to other third parties.

When dealing with the Access Request, you can refuse to release the third-party data unless:

- The third party has consented to the document being released, or

- It is reasonable to disclose the third-party data without consent.

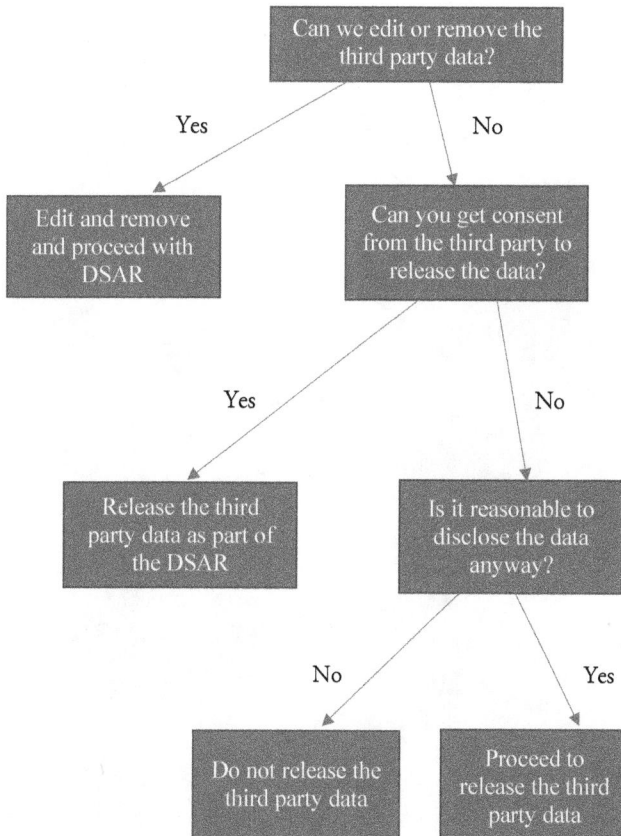

```
              ┌──────────────────────┐
              │ Can we edit or remove the │
              │   third party data?     │
              └──────────────────────┘
         Yes                        No
   ┌────────────────┐      ┌────────────────────┐
   │ Edit and remove │      │ Can you get consent │
   │ and proceed with│      │ from the third party to│
   │     DSAR        │      │  release the data?  │
   └────────────────┘      └────────────────────┘
                    Yes                        No
         ┌──────────────────┐      ┌──────────────────┐
         │ Release the third │      │ Is it reasonable to│
         │ party data as part of│   │  disclose the data │
         │    the DSAR       │      │     anyway?        │
         └──────────────────┘      └──────────────────┘
                              No                    Yes
                 ┌──────────────────┐   ┌──────────────────┐
                 │ Do not release the│   │   Proceed to      │
                 │ third party data  │   │ release the third │
                 └──────────────────┘   │   party data      │
                                        └──────────────────┘
```

CHAPTER SIX
TRAINING STAFF ON
ACCESS REQUESTS

Introduction

To properly deal with subject access requests you must train your company staff on their access Request responsibilities.

Training is one of the most crucial parts of GDPR compliance and Data Subject Access Request Compliance. In fact the ICO says that you should have a system in place for training staff on Access Requests.

Failing to recognise or respond to Access Requests can have severe consequences for your company.

As a company, you must teach your employees about Access Requests and how to manage them.

Training – The Law

Under Article 39 of GDPR, the Data Protection Officer in any company must ensure there is appropriate *"awareness-raising and training of staff involved in processing operations."* [48] This includes training on Access Requests.

The hazards in failing to train

As outlined in Chapter 3, Access Requests can be made in any form including by email or orally. For example, Mary calls her bank's

---

[48] GDPR – Article 39(1)(b)

customer service line. She speaks with Liz at the call centre and makes a verbal access request. Liz has not received any training on Access Requests and fails to recognise that an Access Request has been made. As a result the request is ignored and the bank is in breach of its GDPR obligations. Mary reports the bank to the ICO for infringing her GDPR rights.

General knowledge on Access Requests

All staff should have some general knowledge on Access Requests including:

- **An overview of Access Requests** – Including the definition of Personal Data

- **Consequences of ignoring an Access Request** – Including regulatory fines and legal action.

- **The Rules on DSARs**: ID Verification, Fees, Time limits, Conversing with Agents.

- **Finding the personal data** – Locating the requestor's data, including through the search of emails.

- **Third Party Data** – What to do if there is third party personal data mixed in with the personal data of the requestor.

- **What to do if you receive an Access Request from a customer or a member of staff** – Who to contact and how to escalate this.

- **Our procedures** – Overview of the Company Policy on Access Requests.

The material in this book should help you put some slides together which you can share with all staff members.

What kind of training can we provide to our staff on Access Requests?

There are three types of training:

In-person training – Someone from your organisation or a training provider can come to your office and provide staff with training on Access Requests. The trainer can also provide staff with relevant materials which they can retain and use as a point of reference. This can be a brief training session or it can be a half-day or even a full-day session.

Online Training – You can purchase online training modules on Access Requests for your employees. Your staff members can log on and view the training at their convenience and download the slides from the presentation. You can purchase online modules from service providers.

Training course – Members of staff who are assuming full responsibility for managing the Access Requests in your organisation should ideally take a full 2 or 3-day training course on Access Requests. This will help them with more difficult topics such as locating personal data throughout your organisation and dealing with third-party data.

Who should we train on Access Requests and which topics should we focus on?

a.   **Smaller Firms**

All employees should receive some general knowledge on Access Requests.

If you have a small firm, then I suggest training all of the staff who interact with clients or other individuals (including employees, contractors and any other members of the public). You can show them a short slide presentation of approximately 45 minutes or 1 hour.

You should appoint one person within your company or organisation to deal with Access Requests, if and when they come in. That person should receive much more substantial training on Access Requests, such as a 2 or 3-day course on Access Requests.

For example, let's imagine you own a medical practice. You have appointed the practice manager, Moira, to deal with any Access Requests received from patients. Moira takes a 3-day online training course to help her understand all aspects of Access Requests. At the end of the training course, Moira has a good working knowledge of Access Requests. In particular, Moira knows how to:

- Recognise an Access Request

- Locate the patient data

- Remove any third-party data

- Send the personal data out to the client securely

b.   Larger companies

All employees should receive some general knowledge on Access Requests.

If you are part of a large company then this can form part of your annual training module on Privacy or Data Protection. The content on Access Requests should sit within this module. This can be brief as many of your staff might not interact with the public or ever come into contact with Access Requests.

Some sections of your business are going to need more detailed training, such as Human Resources, IT and the Privacy and Legal Teams because they may be involved in dealing directly with the Access Request. For example, when Sanjeev makes an Access Request to his employer, Big Corp for all of his personal data, the IT

Department are involved in searching for the data, HR are involved in corresponding with Sanjeev about the request and the Privacy and Legal Teams make decisions about whether any legal exemptions apply to the personal data. The personnel in these departments need detailed knowledge of Access Requests.

Below is a table that helps set out the type of training you might want to deliver to staff on Access Requests:

Company Department	Suggested topics in which more detailed training on Access Requests is required
Senior Staff	• Client Access Requests • Employee Access Requests • Legal Professional Privilege and Access Requests (See Chapter 9) • Locating employee data • Redacting employee data
Human Resources	• Employee Access Requests (See Chapter 7) • Legal Professional Privilege and Access Requests • Locating employee data • Redacting employee data

Call Centre staff	<ul><li>How to recognise an Access Request</li><li>How to respond to an Access Request</li><li>Who to notify within your organisation if you receive an Access Request</li></ul>
Client or Public-Facing Staff	<ul><li>How to recognise an Access Request</li><li>How to respond to an Access Request</li><li>Who to notify within your organisation if you receive an Access Request</li></ul>
Information Technology	<ul><li>Locating data for Access Requests</li><li>Searching for personal data in emails</li><li>Searching for data in central and local drives</li><li>Searching for data in applications</li><li>Sending the personal data securely</li></ul>

Remember, not all employees need detailed knowledge on Access Requests. Some departments need more knowledge than others because they will be involved in dealing with Access Requests while others will only need basic knowledge.

Advice on training:

- **Brevity** – Keep training as brief and relevant as you can.

- **Audience engagement** – No-one wants to sit through a tedious and migraine-inducing session on Data Protection. Try to keep it lively with examples and questions for the audience. Using examples of the types of Access Requests your company receives are important. Equally, you should advise your staff on how you usually locate personal data when you receive an Access Request.

- **Tailor it to the audience** – If the training is for Junior Staff, then the training session and the examples should reflect that and have a more conversational tone. Equally, if the training is for more Senior Partners, then a more formal tone would be more appropriate.

- **Record** – It is essential that you keep a record of the training you have conducted. If ever you receive a complaint from the ICO about how you handled an Access Request, the record of that training will be useful in showing the ICO how you have taken Access Requests seriously.

Recap:

- All Staff should receive some in person or online training on Access Requests.

- Some personnel who deal directly with Access Requests will require specific and detailed training.

- The table within this chapter suggests the most appropriate topics for training.

CHAPTER SEVEN
EMPLOYEE ACCESS
REQUESTS

Why are employee Access Requests so difficult?

There are a number of reasons why employee Data Subject Access Requests can be complex and difficult.

- **The sheer volume of personal data** – Employers can accumulate vast quantities of personal data on employees over the years. In one Access Request that ended up in court, the employer had to review 500,000 emails when dealing with the employee's Access Request.[49]

- **The expense** – Employee Access Requests can be expensive. In the above case, the cost of providing access to the employee's data for that one employee was £116,000.

- **Employee requests can be emotionally charged**– Employees rarely make Access Requests when the employment relationship is going well and the emotional element to the case can add an extra layer of complexity.

- **Legal Issues** – Often, when an employee is making an Access Request, they may be considering (or may have already commenced) legal proceedings against the employer. This can add yet more complexity to the Access Request.

---

[49] Deer v University of Oxford [2017] EWCA Civ

A Reminder of the rules on Access Requests

The same rules apply in employee Access Requests as all other Access Requests including:

1. **Access Requests can be made by any means** – An Access Request can be made by any means including by email, letter or orally.

2. **Copy** – Employees are entitled to access their personal data and to have a copy of it.

3. **Within one month** – The employee Request should be processed within one month of receipt of the Request. This can be extended by two further months in the case of complex or numerous requests.

4. **Identity checks** – Reasonable measures can be made to verify the employee's identity (though in practice, these checks are not often as stringent as they are with customers because if you receive an email from the employee from their work email address, then it may be more likely that it is a genuine request).

5. **They can seek all the data their employer holds on them** – Employees can seek all of the personal data relating to them that is held by their employer including years or perhaps even decades of emails.

6. **Third Party Data** – Third Party data such as that of the employee's work colleagues should be edited out of the material released unless those individuals consent to the personal data being released or unless it is reasonable in all the circumstances to release it. This can be complex and costly.

What process should you follow when dealing with employee DSARs?

- **Acknowledge** and **Try to Narrow the Request** – Acknowledge the Access Request from the employee in a letter of response. See if the employee is open to narrowing the scope of the Access Request. (See Template Letter 2, Appendix 1 at the back of this book).

- **Search** – Search relevant locations for your employee data including your systems, databases, applications and paper files.

- **Get the data together** – Collate the personal data that relates to the employee.

- **Review** – Review the data to see if there is any third party data contained therein. See Chapter 5 for more details on Third Party Data.

- **Decide whether to release the Third Party Data** – Decide whether it is appropriate to seek the consent of these individuals before releasing. If you cannot gain consent, then decide whether it is reasonable to release that personal data without consent.

- **Redact** – Redact or remove personal data that should not be disclosed.

- **Consider the exemptions** – Consider whether any of the exemptions may prevent you from releasing personal data to the employee e.g. the rules on confidential references or management forecasting (see Chapter 9).

- **Send it out** – Finalise the data that is to be released to the employee and send it in a secure fashion to the employee.

Are there any exceptions that may prevent us from disclosing personal data to the employee?

There are a number of exemptions on which you may be able to rely that may enable you to withhold certain personal data from an employee who has made an Access Request. The exemptions should only be applied on a case-by-case basis. Always consider the exemptions carefully and take legal advice if you are unsure whether they apply to you.

The table below sets out how some of the exceptions may work in practice in Access Requests made by employees.

Exception	How it could <u>potentially</u> apply to an employee Access Request. These are only examples and you must consider whether they apply to your case.
• Crime and taxation • DPA 2018 – Sch 2, Part 1, Para 2	Peter has made an Access Request to his employer New Lawyers. Peter has been suspected of defrauding the firm. The investigation team have prepared a report on Peter's suspected fraud which they intend to share with the police. New Lawyers do not have to share the report with Peter as part of his Access Request as it may prejudice the investigation. They can provide Peter with the other material unrelated to this investigation as part of his Access Request.

• Management forecasts • DPA 2018 – Sch 2, Part 4, Para 22	Alison, a managing partner, has made an Access Request to her employer, Smart Accountants. Whilst searching for the data, Smart find some emails discussing the fact that Alison and her team are about to be made redundant. Smart do not have to release this information as it *'GDPR provisions do not apply to personal data processed for the purposes of management forecasting or management planning in relation to a business or other activity to the extent that the application of those provisions would be likely to prejudice the conduct of the business or activity concerned.'*
• Negotiations with requestor • DPA 2018 – Sch 2, Part 4, Para 23	Mitt has been negotiating for a pay rise with his employer, a company called Data Lakes Insurance. Whilst negotiations are ongoing, Mitt makes an Access Request. Mitt is not entitled to see the confidential documents in which his manager discusses the maximum sum he would be prepared to pay Mitt because this would prejudice the ongoing negotiations between Mitt and Data Lakes Insurance.

• Legal Professional Privilege • DPA 2018 – Sch 2, Part 4, Para 19	Lucy, an IT professional, has taken a claim against her employer, Cheap Cars. The claim is about to go to court. Just prior to the case arriving in court, Lucy decides to lodge an Access Request with Cheap Cars. Whilst collating the data, Cheap Cars find emails in which Cheap Cars and their lawyers discuss whether they should pay Lucy to settle the case. In the emails, the lawyers also give Cheap Cars legal advice about how to handle Lucy's case. Cheap cars do not disclose these emails because the emails are subject to Legal Professional Privilege.
• Confidential references • DPA 2018 – Sch 2, Part 4, Para 24	Melanie makes an Access Request as she wants to see confidential references given by her old employer to a new employer. Her new employer decides that she is not entitled to see the reference because the reference is subject to the exemption on confidential references.

Please remember that the exemptions should be used sparingly and you must consider them on a case-by-case basis.

Recap:

- Employee Access Requests can be difficult due to the large volumes of data held on employees particularly if they have been employed for many years.

- Employee Access Requests can be emotionally charged and challenging.

- There are a number of exemptions that may apply to some of the personal data relating to employee access requests. This may mean that you do not have to release certain data to an employee if they make an Access Request if that data relates to:

  o Crime and Taxation

  o Management Forecasts e.g. data relating to business forecasting such as redundancies

  o Negotiations e.g. pay negotiations

  o Legal Professional Privilege e.g. data relating to litigation with the employee

  o Confidential references e,g, data relating to employment references relating to the employee

CHAPTER EIGHT
FURTHER RIGHTS
UNDER GDPR

Although Access Requests under GDPR are the most commonly used rights, there are other rights under GDPR. Customers, employees and others can make requests under GDPR based on these rights.

The rights under GDPR are:

1. The Right of Access – The Access Requests we have been dealing with in the previous chapters of this book.

2. The Right to Erasure.

3. The Right to Correct Inaccurate Data.

4. The Right to Restrict Processing.

5. The Right to Data Portability.

6. The Right to Object.

7. The Right to have human oversight in a decision made by a computer.

Most of this book is concerned with Access Requests at 1. above. The rights set out at 2-7 are not as widely used. I will call these rights the 'other rights' for ease of reference.

Below, I set out some of the basic facts relating to the other rights. Then, at the end of this chapter, you will find a brief table, setting out how to apply these other rights. It highlights the actions required for each of the other rights and how they differ from the Access Requests we have been dealing with throughout this book.

The Right to Erasure

Under the Right to Erasure, people have the right to erase their personal data but only in some circumstances.[50]

A person has the right to have their data erased in a number of cases. The main reasons for a person being able to ask you to erase their data are:

- You are processing the person's data based on consent and they have now withdrawn that consent, or

- The data is no longer necessary for the purpose you had originally collected it for, or

- You are processing the personal data for direct marketing purposes and the individual objects to the marketing material, or

- The data has been processed unlawfully by you, for example because you have processed it unfairly or contrary to the law.

See Article 17 for further grounds.

For example, David was a member of The Welsh Hiking Club. He has found the hikes too difficult recently and has left the Club. When David originally joined the Club, they had collected personal data relating to David's health to ensure that they did not recommend hikes that were too strenuous for him. He has now left the Club and he does not want them to have this data. He makes a Right to Erasure request for the Club to delete this data and they agree to do so.

There are a number of exceptions to the Right to Erasure and I describe some of the main exceptions immediately below. This means that a company could refuse to erase the person's data if they required

---

[50] GDPR – Article 17

the data for one of the following reasons:

- Complying with a legal obligation

- To exercise the right of freedom of expression and information

- For the performance of a task carried out in the public interest

- For the establishment, exercise or defence of a legal claim[51]

See Article 17(3) of GDPR for more details on the exceptions to the Right to Erasure.

For an example of the exceptions working in practice let's look at the case of Sarah:

- Sarah took a case against her local council after slipping in a park and injuring her arm.

- Her lawyers, Dodgy & Co., did not issue proceedings in time and Sarah's claim was statute-barred.

- Sarah has taken a professional negligence claim against Dodgy and she has also made an erasure request to Dodgy to delete all her data.

- Dodgy do not have to delete the data as they need it to defend Sarah's legal claim.

If you do receive a Right to Erasure request, you should consider whether the person has a meritorious request. You should also check whether any of the exceptions at Article 17(3) of GDPR apply which would prevent you from deleting the data.

---

[51] GDPR – Article 17(3)

The Right to Correct Personal Data

Under GDPR, individuals have the right to correct inaccurate personal data or to complete incomplete data. This is referred to as the Right to Rectification.

For example, Liliana received access to her records from her optician. She was diagnosed last year by a previous optician as being colour blind. This diagnosis turned out to be incorrect. Liliana has a right to ensure that her records reflect that she is not colour blind. See Article 16 for more details on exercising this right. [52]

It can be difficult if individuals wish to challenge the accuracy of opinion data. It is probably best if the opinion is not removed from the data record as it is subjective and therefore not likely to be 'inaccurate'. A possible option would be to record that the opinion has been challenged.

The Right to Restrict Processing

Under GDPR, individuals have a right to restrict processing.

This right applies in a number of grounds including if:

- the accuracy of the personal data is contested by the data subject and the controller needs to check if the data is accurate, or

- the processing is unlawful and the data subject opposes the complete erasure of the personal data, or

- the controller no longer needs the personal data for the purposes of the processing, but they are required by the data subject for the establishment, exercise or defence of legal

---

[52] GDPR Article 16

claims.

Under this right, individuals can put a temporary hold on the way their personal data is processed until their complaint is resolved. In other words, people can ask you to stop doing whatever it is you are doing with their data whilst their complaint is being resolved.[53]

What does restriction of processing mean? Recital 67 of GDPR says it *"could include…..temporarily moving the selected data to another processing system, making the selected personal data unavailable to users, or temporarily removing published data from a website"*.

If this right applies then very limited data processing can occur. If the restriction is to be lifted, the Controller should advise the data subject of this before the lifting of the restriction occurs. Please see Article 18 of GDPR for the finer detail on the Right to Restrict Processing.

For example. Michelle, a lawyer, sees an article about her and her firm on Legal Cheeky, a website that rates lawyers. Michelle is unsure if the facts of the article are correct and she wants the article taken down whilst she investigates the issue. Legal Cheeky remove the article about Michelle whilst its accuracy is being checked. Legal Cheeky check the accuracy of the article the following week and they are satisfied that it is accurate. Before the article goes back up on the website, Legal Cheeky must contact Michelle to tell her that the restriction on the article is about to end.

The Right to Data Portability

Under GDPR, people have the personal data they have provided to a Controller sent to a new service provider in a 'structured, commonly used and machine-readable format'. In other words, an individual has a potential right to insist that Company A transfers the individual's personal data over to Company B in a manner that the data is easily

---

[53] GDPR – Article 18

usable and accessible by Company B. This right prevents Company A from having a stranglehold over an individual's data and allows the individual to transfer the data to a new service provider like Company B. Company A only has to provide the data to Company B if it is 'technically feasible' to do so.

For this right to apply, the data subject must have provided the data directly to the (rather than the Controller obtaining it from another source such as a third-party company) and the processing must be based on consent or contract.

For example, Denise bought a house 10 years ago. She has been with the same mortgage provider, Pricey Mortgages, for all of that time. Denise wants to move to a new provider called Platinum Mortgages. She asks Pricey to send her data to Platinum. Pricey must transfer the data to Platinum in a 'structured, commonly used and machine-readable format.' This means they must transfer it in a way that is easy for Platinum to use, such as in a CSV file.[54] Please see Article 20 of GDPR for the finer detail on the Right to Data Portability including some of the limits and exceptions to the right.

The Right to Object

Under GDPR, people have the right to object to their data being processed in a number of cases including when it is used for direct marketing. This means they can ask you to stop using their personal information for any marketing purposes, such as sending them marketing emails.[55]

The right to object to marketing is an absolute right and the Controller cannot push back if an individual objects to receiving any more marketing material.

---

[54] GDPR – Article 20

[55] GDPR – Article 21(2)

For example, Rosie received three marketing emails last week from New Lawyers telling Rosie about the services they offer. She is irritated by the frequency of the emails and wants them to stop. She emails New Lawyers telling them she does not want any more marketing communications from them. New Lawyers ensure they do not send Rosie any further marketing emails.

The right to object does not only relate to Marketing material. Individuals can also object to other forms of data processing such as processing for:

- a task carried out in the public interest, or

- the purposes of the data subject's legitimate interests

These objections are not as clear cut as the marketing example. Unlike the objection to marketing described above, the Controller may potentially push back on the data subject's objection to the processing carried out in the public interest or for the data subject's legitimate interests.

Please see Article 21 of GDPR for further detail on the Right to Object.

The Right relating to computer decision making

Under GDPR, people have a right to have human oversight in a decision that has been made by a computer, [56]for example, a decision by a computer that refuses you for a mortgage or refuses your application for a job. For the person to rely on this right, the decision has to be solely by a computer (with no human oversight) and it must significantly affect the person.

The exceptions to this right include where the decision made by the

---

[56] GDPR – Article 22

computer is:

- necessary for the performance of a contract, or

- authorised by law, or

- based on the individual's consent

Where you do want to rely on one of the exceptions to this rule above e.g. where you want a computer to make a decision about a person because you feel you have their consent, then you must ensure that individuals can:

- obtain human oversight or intervention in the decision

- express their point of view

- challenge the decision

For example:

- Riley is a solicitor at Cookstown Lawyers.

- She decides to apply for a promotion to be a partner in the firm. Riley completes an online application form. She enters her details.

- Three weeks later, Riley receives an email telling her that her promotion application has been refused.

- When she asks Cookstown Lawyers about this, they tell her that a computer reviews the applications.

- Riley has a right to ask Cookstown Lawyers to review her promotion application again and this time, to ask a human being to look at the data as well as the computer.

- Cookstown Lawyers must allow Riley to express her views on why she feels she should be promoted.

Please see Article 22 of GDPR for further detail on the Right relating to computer decision making.

Complying with the other rights

As we discussed, most of this book is concerned with Access Requests. The other rights set out above are not as widely used. The table below helps set out the steps you must take if you receive a request relating to one of the GDPR rights.

Type of Right	Time Limit	Form request can be in	Search for the person's personal data	Actions to be taken	Provide a copy of the personal information?	Some of the main exceptions to this right
1. The Right of Access	Within one month	In any form e.g. email or orally	Search all company sources including emails, databases, systems. Ask processors to search too.	Review and consider third party data and whether exceptions apply. Consider Article 15 GDPR.	Provide copy	See Article 12(5) for refusing the request because it is manifestly unfounded or excessive Schedules 2 and 3 of the Data Protection Act 2018
2. The Right to Erasure	Within one month	In any form e.g. email or orally	Search for the data relating to the request ie the data to be deleted	Consider the exceptions. Delete data if appropriate. Consider Article 17 GDPR.	No	See Article 12(5) for refusing the request because it is manifestly unfounded or excessive Article 17(3) Schedules 2 and 3 of the Data Protection Act 2018

3. The Right to Rectification	Within one month	In any form e.g. email or orally	View the data alleged as incorrect.	Consider whether data is inaccurate. Correct or update if necessary. Consider Article 16 GDPR.	No	See Article 12(5) for refusing the request because it is manifestly unfounded or excessive
4. The Right to Restrict processing	Within one month	In any form e.g. email or orally	Consider the request to place a temporary hold on the data.	Consider whether temporary hold is appropriate. Stop processing the data if request is meritorious. Consider Article 18 GDPR.	No	See Article 12(5) for refusing the request because it is manifestly unfounded or excessive Schedules 2 and 3 of the Data Protection Act 2018
5. The Right to Data Portability	Within one month	In any form e.g. email or orally	Search all company sources including emails, databases, systems. Ask processors to search too.	If request has been made out, then put data on commonly used machine-readable file and send to new service provider. Consider Article 20 GDPR.	Provide copy to new service provider	See Article 20(4) See Article 12(5) for refusing the request because it is manifestly unfounded or excessive Schedules 2 and 3 of the Data Protection Act 2018
6. The Right to Object	Within one month	In any form e.g. email or orally	Search for data relating to the request e.g. the Marketing data.	Consider whether objection appropriate. Stop processing the data if request is meritorious. Consider Article 21 GDPR.	No	See Article 12(5) for refusing the request because it is manifestly unfounded or excessive Schedules 2 and 3 of the Data Protection Act 2018

| 7. The Right related to computer decision making | Within one month | In any form e.g. email or orally | Consider whether a computer did make decision without human involvement that significantly affected person. | Ensure human intervention in the decision if appropriate. Consider Article 22 GDPR. | No | Article 22(2) See Article 12(5) for refusing the request because it is manifestly unfounded or excessive |

Recap:

- There are a number of other rights under GDPR including:

  o The Right of Access – The Access Requests we have been dealing with in the previous chapters of this book.

  o The Right to Erasure.

  o The Right to Correct Inaccurate Data.

  o The Right to Restrict Processing.

  o The Right to Data Portability.

  o The Right to Object.

  o The Right to have human oversight in a decision made by a computer.

- These rights are not absolute and are subject to their own exceptions.

- All requests relating to these rights must be dealt with within one month. Requests under these rights can be made in any form including by email, letter or even orally.

CHAPTER NINE
EXEMPTIONS INCLUDING LEGAL PROFESSIONAL PRIVILEGE

Introduction

There are some exceptions (known as "exemptions") to the GDPR rules on Subject Access Requests. These exemptions <u>may</u> allow your company to decline to disclose some information to the requestor.

The ICO has said that companies should not routinely rely on exemptions. Exemptions should be applied sparingly and companies should always lean towards providing as much information to the requestor as possible.

Always be careful in relying on an exemption. Make sure you have a solid legal basis if you intend to rely on one and always check the law carefully and record the decision you have taken. If you are in any doubt about the feasibility of using an exemption, you should take legal advice.

Exemptions are to be applied on a case-by-case basis. You cannot use them in a blanket manner.

Below, I discuss the following exemptions:

- Crime and Taxation

- Legal Professional Privilege (including communications between lawyer and client for the purposes of obtaining legal advice)

- Management information

- Negotiations with the requestor

- Confidential references

Please note that these are mere examples that illustrate how the exemptions <u>may</u> apply. You must consider the facts of the Access Request that you are dealing with and make a judgement on whether the exemption applies in your specific case.

Remember that transparency is one of the main tenets of GDPR. These exemptions should not be used in a manner which is designed to hide personal data from individuals in an unfair or injudicious way.

(5) Crime and Taxation[57]

An insurance company suspects that one of its customers, Jack, has committed fraud by submitting a false claim and they report the issue to the police. During the investigation, Jack makes an Access Request for all his personal data. The company decides not to release the material relating to the investigation to Jack because the data is being processed 'for the detection of crime' and releasing these details to Jack could prejudice the investigation (Data Protection Act 2018, Sch 2, Part 1, para 2). The insurance company do release the other data unrelated to the investigation to Jack including his account details and insurance certificate.

(6) Legal Professional Privilege[58]

This is a complex exemption.

Specifically, this exemption allows you to potentially withhold personal data from release under an Access Request if the data is:

- information in respect of which a claim to legal professional

---

[57] Data Protection Act 2018, Sch 2, Part 1, para 2

[58] Data Protection Act 2018, Sch 2, Part 4, para 19

privilege or, in Scotland, confidentiality of communications, could be maintained in legal proceedings, or

- Information in respect of which a duty of confidentiality is owed by a professional legal adviser to a client of the adviser.

The ICO say:

a) This exemption covers the two branches of legal professional privilege: litigation privilege and legal advice privilege.

b) The English law concept of legal professional privilege encompasses both 'litigation' privilege and 'legal advice' privilege.

c) 'Litigation' privilege applies to confidential communications between a client, professional legal adviser or a third party, but only where litigation is contemplated or in progress.

d) 'Legal advice' privilege only to confidential communications between a client and professional legal adviser for the purpose of seeking or obtaining legal advice.

If the personal data that relate to the Access Request fall within the terms of c) and d) above then you may be able to rely on this exemption.

For example, Alex has taken a claim for discrimination against her employer, World Bank. Prior to the conclusion of the claim, Alex decides to send an Access Request to World Bank for all of her data. Whilst dealing with her Access Request, World Bank find an email in which they and their external lawyers discuss Alex's case. In the email, the lawyers also give World Bank Legal advice about whether to settle Alex's claim. This email does not have to be disclosed because it is 'information in respect of which a claim to legal professional privilege could be maintained in legal proceedings.' (Data Protection Act 2018, Sch 2, Part 4, para 19).

(7) Management Forecasts[59]

Chantelle has made an Access Request to her employer, Coffee World. Whilst collecting the data to send out to her, Coffee World find some emails including one from October 1. The October 1 email discusses Chantelle and the fact that Coffee World might make her redundant next month. Coffee World do not have to release the October 1 email to Chantelle as the Access Request rules 'do not apply to personal data processed for the purposes of management forecasting or management planning in relation to a business or other activity to the extent that the application of those provisions would be likely to prejudice the conduct of the business or activity concerned.' (Data Protection Act 2018, Schedule 2, Part 4, para 22).

(8) Negotiations with the requestor[60]

Sally had an accident at home. She makes a claim on her home insurance policy. Sally has been offered some money by the insurance company to settle the claim before it reaches court. During the negotiations with her insurance company, Sally submits an Access Request to the Insurance company for access to all of her personal data. The insurance company release the data to Sally but they withhold a document containing details of how much the insurance company would pay to settle Sally's claim because the Access Request Rules 'do not apply to personal data that consists of records of the intentions of the controller in relation to any negotiations with the data subject to the extent that the application of those provisions would be likely to prejudice those negotiations.' (Data Protection Act 2018, Schedule 2, Part 4, para 23).

(9) Confidential references[61]

Daniel worked as a manager at Big Cinema but he decided to leave.

---

[59] UK Data Protection Act 2018, Schedule 2, Part 4 para 22

[60] UK Data Protection Act 2018, Schedule 2, Part 4 para 23

[61] UK Data Protection Act 2018, Schedule 2, Part 4 para 24

He applied for a job with Silver Screen Cinemas. Big Cinema provided a confidential reference on Daniel to Silver Screen. Several months later, Daniel makes an Access Request to Silver Screen as he wants to see the reference. The reference does not have to be disclosed to Daniel because the Access Request Rules 'do not apply to personal data consisting of a reference given in confidence for the purposes of employment.' (Data Protection Act 2018, Schedule 2, Part 4, para 24).

Obscure exemptions

There are some further, perhaps more obscure, exemptions relating to:

- Functions designed to protect the public

- Regulatory functions relating to legal services, the health service and children's services

- Judicial appointments, independence and proceedings

- Journalism, academic purposes, artistic purposes

- Archiving in the public interest

- Child abuse data

- Audit functions

- Corporate Finance

- Self-incrimination

- Exam Scripts and Exam Marks[62]

---

[62] ICO Guidance on Subject Access Requests, October 2020, Pages 52, 53

These exemptions may allow a Controller to withhold certain information in relation to an Access Request. Please see ICO Guidance on Subject Access Requests, October 2020, Pages 52-60 for more details.

Also, Data Protection Act 2018, Schedules 2 and 3.

Health Data

There is an exemption to complying with an Access Request for health data to the extent that doing so would be likely to cause serious harm to the physical or mental health of any individual.

If you think this exemption may apply to you, then consider the Data Protection Act 2018, Schedule 3, Part 2 and the ICO Guidance on Subject Access Requests page 64

Education data

There is a specific exemption relating to Education Data. There is an exemption in most cases from providing education data in response to an Access Request to the extent that providing that data would be likely to cause serious harm to the physical or mental health of any individual.

If you think this exemption may apply to you, then consider the Data Protection Act 2018, Schedule 3, Part 4 and the ICO Guidance on Subject Access Requests page 69.

Social work data

There is a specific exemption relating to Social Work Data. There is an exemption in most cases from providing social work data in response to an Access Request to the extent that providing that data

---

and 54

would be likely to cause serious harm to the physical or mental health of any individual.

If you think this exemption may apply to you, then consider the Data Protection Act 2018, Schedule 3, Part 3 and the ICO Guidance on Subject Access Requests page 73.

Recap:

- There are numerous exemptions to Access Requests.

- Exemptions should be used sparingly and on a case by case basis.

- The exemptions may allow you to decline to release certain data as part of your response to an individual's Access Request.

- The main exemptions discussed include Legal Professional Privilege. This exemption covers the two branches of legal professional privilege: litigation privilege and legal advice privilege.

- Further exemptions include management forecasts, crime and taxation, negotiations, confidential references, health data, education data and social work data. There are also many more obscure exemptions.

CHAPTER TEN
FREQUENTLY ASKED QUESTIONS

1. **What is the difference between a Subject Access Request ('Access Request') and a Freedom of Information Request?**

   A Subject Access Request is a request under Article 15 of GDPR. Under this Regulation, an individual can request access to and a copy of the personal data that a company or an organisation holds on them.

   A Freedom of Information Request is a request under the Freedom of Information (FOI) Act 2000. Under this law, a member of the public can request information from public authorities that has been recorded by these authorities. The FOI Act does not give people access to their own personal data (information about themselves). If a member of the public wants to see information that a public authority holds about them, they should make a Subject Access Request.

2. **What is personal data?**

   The right to access relates to "personal data".

   Article 4(1) of GDPR states that 'personal data' means:

   a. any information

   b. relating to an identified or identifiable natural person ('data subject').

   A company may hold personal data about you in many shapes and sizes including data relating to your name, address, email address, bank card information, purchase history, online browsing activity and preferences. It might also hold CCTV footage of you and call recording data.

3. **Why does the ICO receive so many complaints about Access Requests?**

The ICO receives more complaints from individuals about Access Requests than any other topic. In their 2021/2022 Annual report, complaints about Access Requests accounted for 37% of all complaints. In the author's view, Access Requests cause so many complaints because: Often companies have substandard processes in place for dealing with Access Requests and this can cause annoyance with individuals who believe their Access Requests are not being complied with adequately or at all.

4. **Must an Access Request be made in any particular form?**

A person can make an Access Request in any form including by email, letter, social media message or even orally. The request does not have to say that it is a Subject Access Request, nor does it have to mention GDPR.

See Chapter 3.

5. **Can I ask the client to complete our company Subject Access Request Form when they are submitting their Access Request?**

You can ask. However, they do not have to complete your form.

See Chapter 3.

6. **How should I send the personal data out to the person making the request?**

If the request is made by email, then the response should be sent out by email (Article 12(3) GDPR). If the person requests the information to be provided orally, then you should provide it orally (Article 12(1) GDPR).

See Chapter 3.

7. **How long does a company have to comply with an Access Request?**

A response must be provided within one month of receipt of the request. The time limit may be extended by a further two months if the requests are numerous or complex. (Article 12(3) GDPR).

See Chapter 3.

8. **Must I find every scrap of personal data on the requestor if they make an Access Request?**

The UK case of Deer v. Oxford University sheds light on this subject [63]. In this case, Lord Justice Lewison said:

> "*the implied obligation to search…is limited to a reasonable and proportionate search….. the result of a search does not necessarily mean that every item of personal data relating to an individual will be retrieved*".

See Chapter 4 for more details on this.

9. **How do I ensure the Access Request is genuine?**

You should use "*all reasonable measures*"[64] to verify the identity of the requestor to make sure it is a genuine request. If you know the person well, for example, if it is an employee making the request, then you may not need significant identity checks. However, if it

---

[63] Deer-v-University of Oxford [2017] EWCA (Civ) 121

[64] GDPR – Recital 64

is a customer or someone with whom you have a limited relationship, deeper identity checks will be needed.

See Chapter 3.

10. **Why do companies dislike Access Requests so much?**

They can be very expensive. In the case of Deer (see 7. above), the requestor was a long-standing employee and made a request against their employer. 500,000 emails had to be reviewed and the Access Request was estimated to have cost the employer £116,000. Also, Access Requests can take considerable time and they can be both stressful and controversial.

11. **Does the requestor need a good reason to make an Access Request?**

No. Anyone can ask a company to confirm whether it processes their personal data and request access to and a copy of that personal data. The requestor's motive for making the request is irrelevant. See Chapter 2.

12. **Can I request other data over and above my personal data in an Access Request?**

No. An Access Request only allows you to access your own personal data. See Chapter 1.

13. **Can companies charge a fee for complying with Subject Access Requests?**

Ordinarily no. Fees can be charged by companies for 'administrative costs' such as copying, postage and printing if the Access Request is manifestly unfounded or excessive (Article 12(5) GDPR). Charging fees for Access Requests is probably more trouble than it is worth.

14. **Can you release personal data relating to someone else in an Access Request?**

Let's say Person 1 makes an Access Request. During the search, documents are found that mention Person 1 and Person 2. It is best to try to remove references to Person 2. If that is not possible, then you can ask Person 2 for their permission to release Person 2's personal data as part of Person 1's Access Request. If you are unable to obtain their permission, then you must ask whether it is reasonable in the circumstances to release Person 2's data as part of the request.

See Chapter 5.

15. **What are the consequences of failing to comply with Access Request obligations?**

You can be fined by an EU Data Protection Regulator (known as a 'Supervisory Authority') for any breach of GDPR, including breaches of the Access Request provisions. You may also be sued by the person making the Access Request. Under section 173 of the Data Protection Act 2018, it is a criminal offence to alter, deface, block, erase, destroy or conceal information with the intention of preventing disclosure of all or part of the information that the person making the request would have been entitled to receive.

See Chapter 1.

16. **Can a company force an individual to make an Access Request?**

No. It is a criminal offence to force an individual to make an Access Request for their records e.g. if a prospective employer forces a candidate to make an access request to another organisation for their criminal record so that the prospective employer can see it.[65]

17. What should companies do to prepare for Access Requests?

Companies should put systems and controls in place to deal with Access Requests such as policies and procedures (see the Chapter 6 in this book on 'Training' and the later appendix on 'Policies and Procedures').

18. Can individuals use Access Requests to put pressure on companies to deal with their complaint?

Yes. The motive of the person is irrelevant when dealing with Access Requests and the UK courts have confirmed this. In other words, an individual may not have good intentions towards your company and may be using the Access Request to gain leverage over your company but this will not prevent the individual from asserting their Right to Access their personal data. However, your company may be able to refuse to comply with an Access Request if it is manifestly unfounded or manifestly excessive. The ICO has said that if an Access Request is malicious or is being used to harass an organisation then the organisation can refuse to deal with the request. See Chapter 3 for more details.

---

[65] Data Protection Act 2018, section 184

APPENDIX ONE
TEMPLATES FOR RESPONDING
TO ACCESS REQUESTS

Introduction – This appendix contains template responses to help you deal with Access Requests. These include:

- An acknowledgment of receipt of the Access Request.

- A template asking the requestor to narrow their request.

- A template advising the requestor that the Access Request will be delayed.

- A template saying you are refusing to act on the request.

- A template to your suppliers/processors asking them to help you locate personal data.

- A template to other departments within your company asking them to help you locate personal data.

- A template to third parties asking them for consent to release the personal data relating to the third party to the individual making the access request.

- A template releasing the personal data to the data subject.

TEMPLATE 1 – Email acknowledgement of a Data Subject Access Request and identity verification

Dear [enter name],

Thank you for your Data Subject Access Request under Article 15 of GDPR which we received by [enter post/email/phone] on [enter date].

We are currently dealing with your request.

We aim to have fully responded to your Data Subject Access Request by [enter data within one month of receipt]. If we require an extension to this time limit, we will write to advise you of this before that date.

We would also ask that you complete our Data Subject Access Template Request Form. You are under no obligation to complete the form but completing it will help us in locating your data and providing a more efficient response to you.

[We require proof of identity from you in order to process your request including the following documents [Delete as appropriate]]:

- Customer ID

- Account number

- Copy of driving licence/passport/national insurance number

- Copy of Utility Bill with your name and address

- Employee ID

- Former employee email address

- Employment dates (start and end)

Please submit your documentation and your Data Subject Access Request Form via [enter e.g. email address].

Yours etc.

Data Subject Access Request form

Name	
Address	
Email Address	
Phone Number	
Date of Birth	
Client Number	
Description of Services we provided to you	
Names of our staff members /locations of offices with which you were in contact	
Approximate date on which you commenced using our services	
Description of the data you are seeking from us e.g. • Employment records (please include the relevant dates) • Email correspondence (please specify the senders/recipients along with the subject lines along with the relevant dates)	

• Invoices (please include the relevant dates) • Billing records (please include the relevant dates) • Details of further personal data requested by you	
Signed by Data Subject:	
Signed by Agent for Data Subject:	
Date:	

TEMPLATE 2 – Email asking the requestor to narrow the search

Dear [enter name],

Thank you for your Data Subject Access Request under Article 15 of GDPR which we received by [enter post/email/phone] on [enter date].

We are currently locating your personal data.

GDPR Recital 63 states *"the controller should be able to request that, before the information is delivered, the data subject specify the information or processing activities to which the request relates."*

Please provide us with the following information so we can deal with your request:

- The types of documents you seek [e.g. your file, email correspondence, payment records]

- The types of data processing you seek further details on [professional advice you were given, marketing information relating to you]

- The relevant dates relating to these documents [e.g. between January 2018 and March 2018]

- Further information [enter further missing information that you require either to identify the data subject or process the request]

We aim to have fully responded to your Data Subject Access Request by [enter date]. If we require an extension to this time limit, we will write to advise you of this by [enter date].

Yours etc.

TEMPLATE 3 – As we discussed in Chapter 3, the one-month time limit for Access Requests can be extended by two months where necessary taking into account the complexity and number of requests. This is an email template outlining that the Access Request will be delayed on that basis.

Dear [enter name],

Thank you for your Data Subject Access Request under Article 15 of GDPR which we received by [enter post/email/phone] on [enter date].

Ordinarily, we try to ensure Data Subject Access Requests are processed within one month.

However, in accordance with Article 12(3) of GDPR, we require more time [enter reason relating to the complexity or number of requests e.g. we are trying to locate personal data stored on our archives and multiple systems/you have made a number of related requests that will take time to collate/you have asked for a large volume of personal data going back many years].

We will be in a position to provide your personal data by the [enter date within three months of receipt of the Access Request].

Yours etc.

TEMPLATE 4 – As we discussed in Chapter 3, Access Requests can be refused in some cases if the request is manifestly unfounded or manifestly excessive. This template email advises that you are refusing to act on an Access Request.

Dear [enter name],

Thank you for your Data Subject Access Request under Article 15 of GDPR which we received by [enter post/email/phone] on [enter date].

Ordinarily, we try to ensure DSARs are processed within one month.

However, in accordance with Article 12(5) of GDPR, we are refusing to act and to deal with your Data Subject Access Request(s). The reason we have taken this position is because [enter reason relating to the request being manifestly unfounded or excessive e.g. we believe you are using the process to cause disruption/we believe your requests to be excessive in that they repeat the substance of previous requests].

This is evidenced by [enter details of evidence e.g. your request has made unsubstantiated allegations/you have made multiple requests on the same issue].

You have a right to complain to the Information Commissioner's Office or to seek legal advice if you have an issue with the manner in which your personal data has been processed.

Yours etc.

TEMPLATE 5 – Letter to agent acting on behalf of requestor

Name and address of Agent   Date

Dear Sirs,

Thank you for your [email/letter/communication] of [enter date] in which you state you are acting on behalf of the Data Subject [enter name] and further stating that you wish to make a Data Subject Access request under Article 15 of GDPR in respect of this Data Subject.

We require evidence of your legal authority to act on behalf of this Data Subject [*unless the agent is a lawyer in which case you should assume they have the appropriate authority*].

Please provide the following documentation [delete as appropriate].

- A letter of authority signed by the Data Subject.

- [Enter further appropriate document]

Please submit your documentation via [email/via our secure portal].

[[We require clarification on the data you are seeking: please specify [the specific documents you are seeking/dates relating to these documents]]

Please also complete our Access Request form below **on behalf of the requestor** so that we can deal with this request efficiently.

Yours etc.

Data Subject Access Request form

Name of data subject	
Address	
Email Address	
Phone Number	
Date of Birth	
Client Number	
Description of Services we provided to your client	
Names of our staff members /locations of offices with whom your client was in contact	
Approximate date on which your client commenced using our services	
Description of the data your client are seeking from us e.g.	

• Employment records (please include the relevant dates) • Email correspondence (please specify the senders/recipients along with the subject lines along with the relevant dates) • Invoices (please include the relevant dates) • Billing records (please include the relevant dates) • Details of further personal data requested by you	
Signed by Data Subject:	
Signed by Agent for Data Subject:	
Date:	

TEMPLATE 6 – Template email to Processors/suppliers seeking assistance on finding personal data that relates to an Access Request that you received as a Controller

Dear [enter contact name],

We require your assistance. We are a Data Controller and we received a Data Subject Access Request from a Data Subject [customer/employee/marketing prospect/patient] under Article 15 of GDPR.

We require your assistance as our Data Processor in locating this personal data as you are obliged to do under your contract.

Please provide all the personal data you hold on this individual on our behalf including [electronic, paper, CCTV, call recordings etc] within the next [7/14 days].

Yours etc.

TEMPLATE 7 – Template email to other internal departments in your organisation seeking assistance on finding personal data that relates to an Access Request that you received as a Controller

Dear [enter name of person from relevant department e.g. IT/HR/Marketing/Billing],

We require your assistance. As you know, our firm is a Data Controller under the GDPR and we received a Data Subject Access Request from a Data Subject [customer/employee/marketing prospect] under Article 15 of GDPR.

The Data Subject's name is [enter name] and they can also be identified from the following information [enter client number/date of birth etc].

We believe your department can help us locate the personal data relating to this data subject and we require your assistance with this matter.

Please search the following areas [delete as appropriate]:

- Email databases

- Call recordings

- Client files

- Paper records

- Billing records

We are under strict time limits to provide this information to the individual as set down by GDPR. Please provide all the personal data you hold on this individual within the next [7 days].

Please note that this matter is highly confidential.

Yours etc.

TEMPLATE 8 – As discussed in Chapter 5, sometimes the personal data of a third party can be mixed in with data relating to the person making the Access Request. In other words, Person A's Data may be mixed up with the personal data of Person B. We may seek consent from Person B to release their data to Person A. This is a template email to third party requesting consent relating to the release of third-party data.

Dear [enter name],

We require your assistance. We received a Subject Access Request from a Data Subject under Article 15 of GDPR. The Data Subject seeks Access to the personal data we hold on them.

Whilst preparing our response, we found personal data relating to the Data Subject which is mixed with personal data relating to you. The details of this personal data are [enter details e.g. an email sent by you to the Data Subject on 1st April discussing the Data Subject's job performance].

We are seeking your consent to release this data to the Data Subject notwithstanding that it also contains information about you.

We are under strict time limits to provide this information to the individual as set down by GDPR. Please respond within the next [7 days].

Please note that this matter is highly confidential.

Yours etc.

TEMPLATE 9 – Letter releasing the Personal Data to the Data Subject

Dear [enter name],

Thank you for your Data Subject Access Request under Article 15 of GDPR which we received by [enter post/email/phone] on [enter date].

You requested [delete as appropriate; a copy of all your personal data/your emails from [enter dates]/a copy of your personal data and a copy of the supplementary information set out at Article 15 of GDPR].

The security of your personal data is important to us. We hereby provide your personal data [Delete as appropriate] in this envelope which was sent by secure mail / through our online portal which may be accessed using the following instructions/ via secure email in a password protected document.

[PLEASE COMPLETE THE TABLE BELOW FOR THE DATA SUBJECT IF THEY HAVE ASKED FOR THE SUPPLEMENTARY INFORMATION AS SET OUT BELOW. THIS TABLE IS ONLY REQUIRED IF YOU HAVE BEEN ASKED BY THE REQUESTOR FOR THE SUPPLEMENTARY INFORMATION AT GDPR ARTICLE 15 1(A)-(H). SEE CHAPTER 2 FOR MORE DETAILS]

Supplementary Information	Our answer
a. The purposes of our processing i.e. why we are doing the processing;	We process your personal data for the following purposes:
b. The categories of personal data concerned i.e. the types of personal data elements we are processing;	The categories of data on you we process include: e.g. • Client information • Payment details • Online tracking information
c. The recipients or categories of recipient we disclose the personal data to i.e. information about who we are sharing the personal data with;	The recipients of this data include: e.g. • IT support • Marketing companies who process data on our behalf • Cloud providers
d. The retention period for storing the personal data or, where this is not possible, the criteria for determining how long we will store it i.e. how long we are keeping the personal data before deleting it;	Your data is retained for the following length of time:

e. The existence of their right to request rectification, erasure or restriction or to object to such processing i.e. the other rights they are entitled to assert under GDPR (See Chapter 8)	You do have a right to make those requests to us in respect of your personal data. Please submit a request to [enter appropriate company email address for GDPR requests]
f. The right to lodge a complaint with the ICO or another supervisory authority;	You have a right to make a complaint to the ICO.
g. Information about the source of the data, where it was not obtained directly from the individual i.e. where or from whom did we obtain the data.	In respect of the personal data we hold on you that we did not collect from you directly, this data was collected from: e.g. • Cookies • When you completed our client form • When you gave instructions to us about your case • From third party databases [enter details] • From the following processors [enter details]

h. The existence of automated decision-making (including profiling) i.e. whether any computer is making a decision about the data subject and what the logic is relating to this	We conduct the following automated decision making involving the processing of your e.g. job application, etc. This program works in the following way [enter details e.g. the computer program rates candidates on the basis of their years or experience in the profession] OR We do not use automated decision making with your personal data.
i. The safeguards we provide if we transfer personal data to a country outside the EU or international organisation i.e. whether we are sending the personal data outside the EU or UK.	We use the following safeguards to ensure safe transfer of your data e.g. Contractual Clauses between us and the receiving company ensure the safety of your personal data.

You have further rights under GDPR including the right to rectify or erase certain elements of your data or to move your data to a new service provider.

You have a right to complain to the Information Commissioner's Office or to seek legal advice if you have an issue with the manner in which your personal data has been processed.

APPENDIX TWO
ACCESS REQUEST POLICIES
AND PROCEDURES

Introduction

Companies must put systems and controls in place to deal with Access Requests. In particular, training and policies are important in dealing with Access Requests. In this appendix we set out why staff policies are essential in dealing with Access Requests and we include a template policy that you may wish to use in order to help you draft your own internal staff policy on this subject. A staff policy is an internal staff facing document that sets out the rules of the game in terms of dealing with Access Requests.

It is important that you have policies and procedures in place to allow your company to deal with Data Subject Access Requests.

This is important for 3 reasons:

- **Staff** – Your staff must know what the rules are in terms of dealing with Subject Access Requests.

- **Organisation** – Policies and procedures help you manage and organise large volumes of Access Requests coming in.

- **Consistency** – They also help you to deal with Access Requests and personal data in a manner that is consistent and reduces the potential for mistakes.

What kind of staff policy should we put in place?

The Personal Data Request Policy is a high-level document that sets out the responsibility on staff to comply with Access Requests and other Personal Data Requests such as the Right to Erasure, The Right to Data Portability etc.

SUGGESTED TEMPLATE – You might find the below template policy useful if you wish to draft a policy on Access Requests for your company.

STAFF DATA SUBJECT REQUEST POLICY

Definitions

Personal data is any information relating to an identifiable Data Subject.

A Data Subject is any human being to whom the personal data relates.

This policy applies to all employees, contractors and agents ('Staff') at this company [enter name of company]. Any breach of this policy could lead to disciplinary action.

The General Data Protection Regulation (GDPR) and other Data Protection Laws and Regulations allow individuals certain rights over their personal data. These Requests are called Data Subject Requests ('Requests').

This Policy details the steps we will take to deal with these Requests from individuals.

When we deal with these Requests, we will:

- *Act in a fair, lawful and transparent manner*

- *Comply with the rules on personal data security and time limits*

- *Respect the rights of all people*

Failure to comply with this Policy could lead to regulatory sanctions, litigation and reputational damage and could cause loss and damage to individuals.

Individuals have a right to:

- *Access and to be given a copy of their personal data*

- *Erase their personal data*

- *Correct their personal data*

- *Move their personal data to a new service provider*

Individuals making Data Subject Requests

Under the law, individuals can make Data Subject Requests by:

- *Emailing us at [enter email address for Access Requests e.g. Dataprotectionofficer@yourcompany.com]*

- *Advising a member of our staff on the telephone*

- *Letter*

- *Other means, such as via social media*

Requests may be made by any individual including customers, employees and other members of the public.

Oversight of Data Subject Requests within our company

[Enter name of person] from [enter name of department in which person works] has responsibility for managing and processing any Requests as they come in. All staff are responsible for recognising Data Subject Requests and escalating them to [enter name of person] on the day they are received.

Time Limits

When we receive a Data Subject Request, we will ensure it is processed without delay and at the very least within one month of receipt of the request. The time limit may be extended by a further two months if the request is complex or if we receive multiple requests from the same person.

Identification

This company will seek additional information necessary to verify the identity of any person making a Request if we have reasonable doubts about the identity of the person making the request.

Type of requestor	Means of Verification
☐ Client	• Customer ID; or • Account number; and • Utility Bill
☐ Individual with whom we have no direct relationship e.g. a marketing prospect or a third-party individual on whom we hold personal data	• Copy of driving licence or passport; and • Utility Bill with individual's name and address
☐ Former Employee	• Employee ID; and • Former employee email address; and • Employment dates (start and end)

| ☐ Current Employee | • Email Access Request; and |
| | • Follow up phone call to check |

Records

We will retain records of all Requests received. In particular, we will track:

- *Data Subject Name*

- *ID Verification*

- *Request Date*

- *Request Type (Access, Erasure)*

- *Assigned Employee(s)*

- *Request Status (New, In Progress, Closed)*

- *Format*

Responding to requests

Annexed to this Policy are some Template Letters of Response which we use to communicate with the Data Subject throughout the Data Subject Request procedure.

When we receive a Data Subject Request, we will send an email of acknowledgement to the Data Subject.

Further emails may follow from us including:

- *Email asking the Data Subject to narrow the search in an Access*

Request

- *Email advising that we are refusing to act on an Access Request*

- *Email to agent acting on behalf of Data Subject*

- *Email to Processors seeking assistance on Data Subject Access Request*

- *Email releasing the Personal Data to the Data Subject in an Access Request*

Data Access Requests

We will endeavour to give Data Subjects access to and a copy of their personal data.

Searching for personal data

After receiving a Data Subject Request, searches should be made for all relevant personal data relating to the request within our company including in databases, systems and applications. We will also request assistance from Outsourced Processors, where appropriate.

Reviewing the personal data

Once the personal data is collated, [enter name] will review the personal data and redact any information that is not appropriate to provide to the requestor. These redactions may include third party data and other information that may not be disclosable.

Third Party Data

All third-party data will be deleted or removed from any personal data that we send out in a Request unless it is not feasible to do so in which case we will:

- **Consent** – Seek the consent of the third party before the data is released.

- **Reasonable** – If this is not possible, we will consider whether it is reasonable in the circumstances to release the personal data relating to the third party.

Exceptions

We will consider whether any exception applies to the personal data we are reviewing, including within the areas of:

- Crime and taxation

- Legal professional privilege

- Management information

- Negotiations with the requestor

- Confidential references

These issues may have an impact on whether the personal data is disclosed.

Sending the personal data out

Personal data will be sent out in a form and manner that is legible and clear. If necessary, explanations will be provided so that the Data Subject understands the personal data.

When sending the personal data out, we will ensure that appropriate steps are taken to ensure the personal data is secure.

Data Rectification Requests

A Data Subject can make a request for us to rectify their personal data. In receiving such a request, we will consider applicable law and regulation and take steps to fulfil the request where it is appropriate to do so.

Erasure requests

A Data Subject can make a request for us to erase their personal data. In receiving such a request, we will consider applicable law and regulation and take steps to fulfil the request where it is appropriate to do so.

Portability requests

A Data Subject can make a request for us to move their personal data to a new service provider. In receiving such a request, we will consider applicable law and regulation and take steps to fulfil the request where it is appropriate to do so.

Objection requests

A Data Subject can object to their personal data being processed. In receiving such a request, we will consider applicable law and regulation and take steps to fulfil the request where it is appropriate to do so.

Further information

The person responsible for Access Requests in the organisation is (enter name, email address and job title). Please contact this person if you have any questions about Access Requests.

Automated Processing Requests

A Data Subject can make a request not to be subject to automated processing. In receiving such a request, we will consider applicable law and regulation and take steps to fulfil the request where it is appropriate to do so.

Version History

Author

Date

_____*END OF TEMPLATE POLICY*_____

Now that we have considered the template Access Request Policy, the remainder of this appendix will look at some other aspects for us to consider in relation to Access Request policies.

Having procedures that staff understand

Policies and procedures are useless if staff do not read or use them.

It is important that your staff understand where to find the Staff Data Subject Request Policy. It is always a good idea to put it on your internal company intranet page.

You can make the slides from your Data Protection Training available on your internal staff intranet page so that Staff can look at these if they need any more information on how to deal with a Data Subject Access Request.

Sending out a company communication to employees explaining what the Policy is and what it does, helps embed the policy.

Helping people understand how to make Access Requests

Why would we want to do that? Won't it encourage them to make these requests?

When a person wants to make an Access Request, they will usually go ahead and make one. Having a process in place that allows people to make Access Requests is sensible because it means you can have a certain amount of control and consistency in respect of the requests you are managing.

For all companies, it pays to set out clearly the procedure by which individuals can make an Access Request. In your Internet Privacy Notice (the notice on your public webpage explaining how you process personal data), you can have a section that explains to individuals how to make an Access Request. You can provide contact details to allow them to do so.

You might say in your Privacy Notice:

You have the following rights in respect of your personal data:

- *The right to be informed about how we process your data.*

- *The right of access to your data and to receive a copy of the data.*

- *The right to rectification of your data if you believe it is inaccurate.*

- *The right to erasure certain elements of your personal data.*

- *The right to restrict processing of your data in some cases.*

- *The right to move your data to a new provider in some cases.*

- *The right to object to your data being processed in some cases.*

- *Rights in relation to automated decision making and profiling i.e. the right to stop computers from making decisions about you.*

If you wish to assert any of these rights, then please contact us at [enter email address of person who deals with Data Subject Requests].

Some very high-tech companies have systems in place which allow Data Subjects to access and download their personal data directly via an online system. This is encouraged in GDPR Recital 63 which says that "*Where possible, the controller should be able to provide remote access to a secure system which would provide the data subject with direct access to his or her personal data*".

Recap:

- Having internal staff facing policies in place is an important part of Access Request compliance

- Policies should be clear and easy to understand

- The template policy in this appendix can be used to help guide you – This policy sets out the rules for employees on access requests, the definitions, the rules on ID verification as well as the point of contact for Access Requests in the company

MORE BOOKS BY
LAW BRIEF PUBLISHING

A selection of our other titles available now:-

'A Practical Guide to Parental Alienation in Private and Public Law Children Cases' by Sam King QC & Frankie Shama
'Contested Heritage – Removing Art from Land and Historic Buildings' by Richard Harwood QC, Catherine Dobson, David Sawtell
'The Limits of Separate Legal Personality: When Those Running a Company Can Be Held Personally Liable for Losses Caused to Third Parties Outside of the Company' by Dr Mike Wilkinson
'A Practical Guide to Transgender Law' by Robin Moira White & Nicola Newbegin
'Artificial Intelligence – The Practical Legal Issues (2nd Edition)' by John Buyers
'A Practical Guide to Residential Freehold Conveyancing' by Lorraine Richardson
'A Practical Guide to Pensions on Divorce for Lawyers' by Bryan Scant
'A Practical Guide to Challenging Sham Marriage Allegations in Immigration Law' by Priya Solanki
'A Practical Guide to Legal Rights in Scotland' by Sarah-Jane Macdonald
'A Practical Guide to New Build Conveyancing' by Paul Sams & Rebecca East
'A Practical Guide to Defending Barristers in Disciplinary Cases' by Marc Beaumont
'A Practical Guide to Inherited Wealth on Divorce' by Hayley Trim
'A Practical Guide to Practice Direction 12J and Domestic Abuse in Private Law Children Proceedings' by Rebecca Cross & Malvika Jaganmohan
'A Practical Guide to Confiscation and Restraint' by Narita Bahra QC, John Carl Townsend, David Winch
'A Practical Guide to the Law of Forests in Scotland' by Philip Buchan
'A Practical Guide to Health and Medical Cases in Immigration Law' by Rebecca Chapman & Miranda Butler
'A Practical Guide to Bad Character Evidence for Criminal Practitioners by Aparna Rao
'A Practical Guide to Extradition Law post-Brexit' by Myles Grandison et al

These books and more are available to order online direct from the publisher at www.lawbriefpublishing.com, where you can also read free sample chapters. For any queries, contact us on 0844 587 2383 or mail@lawbriefpublishing.com.

Our books are also usually in stock at www.amazon.co.uk with free next day delivery for Prime members, and at good legal bookshops such as Wildy & Sons.

We are regularly launching new books in our series of practical day-to-day practitioners' guides. Visit our website and join our free newsletter to be kept informed and to receive special offers, free chapters, etc.

You can also follow us on Twitter at www.twitter.com/lawbriefpub.

www.ingramcontent.com/pod-product-compliance
Lightning Source LLC
Chambersburg PA
CBHW070733220326
41598CB00024BA/3409